MUSICA FICTA

(Figures of Wagner)

MERIDIAN

Crossing Aesthetics

Werner Hamacher

& David E. Wellbery

Editors

Translated by
Felicia McCarren

*Stanford
University
Press*

*Stanford
California
1994*

MUSICA FICTA

(Figures of Wagner)

Philippe Lacoue-Labarthe

Assistance for the translation was
provided by the French Ministry of Culture

Musica Ficta (Figures of Wagner) was
originally published in French in 1991 under the
title *Musica Ficta (Figures de Wagner)*.
© 1991 by Christian Bourgois Editeur

To Gérard Genette, who is here in accord.

Contents

Translator's Foreword   xi

Preface   xv

§ 1 Baudelaire   1

§ 2 Mallarmé   41

§ 3 Heidegger   85

§ 4 Adorno   117

Notes   147

Translator's Foreword

This is not a book about opera, or even strictly "about" music. It is rather a timely meditation on music—specifically the lyric mode of opera—as a site for discussion of the more general aesthetic program called Wagnerism. Sounding philosophy's dialogue—or lack of one—with music, Lacoue-Labarthe opens up a new space for consideration of the lyric subject, music and representation,[1] and what he has elsewhere called the "fiction" of the political. These issues, treated here in specific historical sequence and precise philosophical context, are still with us.

Opera is, once again, flourishing in the West, with opera houses filling in what John Rockwell has recently called the "black holes" in "the nearly unbroken sweep of operatic history from 1600 to modernity."[2] Aficionados say that opera's currency has never waned, but new productions and new opera houses in France illustrate opera's regained predominance. Projects within the Ministry of Culture and without have focused on producing and promoting the French repertory, and less frequently performed French works from the baroque to the twentieth century are now being

1. For work on this dialogue inspired by Lacoue-Labarthe, see Susan Bernstein, "Fear of Music? Nietzsche's Double Vision of the 'Musical Feminine,'" in Peter J. Burgard, ed., *Nietzsche and the Feminine* (Charlottesville: University Press of Virginia, 1994).

2. *New York Times*, 27 December 1993, 1(B).

staged by French and non-French directors. Nowhere is this resurgence of opera so apparent as in the Place de la Bastille, one of the cultural foci of Paris in the last decade and the site of perhaps the most audacious of the government's *Grands Travaux*, the Opéra de la Bastille. Planting a new opera house in one of the most popular and animated quarters of Paris means assuming that opera still defines a political style as much as museums, libraries, and grand arches do; it means assuming that opera is still at the center of people's lives and that it still carries a social and political charge. "750,000 spectators will go to the Paris Opéra next season," reads the 1993–94 season's advertisement; "*Why not you?*" Not since Louis-Désiré Véron, director of the Paris Opéra after the July Revolution of 1830, heightened demand for tickets by turning would-be buyers away from the box office, certain of their redoubled return, has the attempt to build an audience through the strategies of mimetism been so apparent. The 1993–94 season opened with a production of Wagner's *Flying Dutchman* directed by Werner Herzog, and this season Paris awaits the first *Ring* cycle to be staged there in years.

Although this is not a book "about" Wagner, music practice does, in fact, hold a place here. Lacoue-Labarthe is both music lover and philosopher; the progression of scenes charts Lacoue-Labarthe's own course, as he notes in his preface. When asked what place Wagner held in his musical taste before the critical distance developed and analyzed in Chapters 2, 3, and 4, the author describes the same emotional investment of Baudelaire in Chapter 1: "I made the pilgrimage" to Bayreuth. Baudelaire's passion for Wagner's music is not, then, criticized in retrospect but weighed in context, in much the same way that the educated opera lover may reject Wagner's writing but is always moved by one motif or another.

Thus, scenes that replay those made over or about Wagner and studied in this book surface in today's music world, with variations or reversals worth noting.

§ Nineteenth-century literature in thrall to musical form is the image created by Baudelaire's reaction to Wagner: "In you I found everything—I found myself." Institutionalized in literary study via Walter Pater's fin-de-siècle formulation about the arts constantly aspiring to the condition of music, this trend is reversed in late-twentieth-century academic discussion between literary theorists and musicologists, in which the critical discourse of theory becomes the language both sides seek to speak, as if all arts were now aspiring to the condition of theory.

§ The Metropolitan Opera in New York, the last holdout among opera houses in this country, considers giving in to the trend of projecting supertitles above the stage, despite arguments that it takes attention away from the performance and divides the audience by causing those who do not know the libretto to laugh at the wrong time. Met conductor James Levine, himself a performer (at one concert he changed costume six times for the six Brandenburg concerti), says, "Over my dead body will they show those things at this house. I cannot imagine not wanting the audience riveted on the performers at every moment."[3]

§ Loaded with nineteenth-century connotation, "opera" becomes a bad word for some composers; asked if he will write another opera (after *Le Grand Macabre*, almost exclusively performed as a concert opera), Transylvanian composer György Ligeti says "No, not an opera. Maybe something I would call a music-drama." Opera in every way but in name. But if "opera" is a bad word for this sometime Hungarian, sometime Romanian composer now living in Hamburg, it is not so for Herbert Zipper, a composer and conductor born in Austria roughly a generation before Ligeti. National Socialism confiscated and destroyed his music and sent the composer to Dachau, but it could not destroy the musical impulse.[4] A few pieces preserved by copyists and pupils—but more significantly the political activism through music education which has been his life's work in Dachau, in the United States, the Philippines, Europe, and China—provide an alternative example of the continuing power of music both against historical politics and within political history.

§ And finally, in an interesting take on the "caesura" of Hölderin cited by Adorno to speak about Schönberg's *Moses and Aaron*, Lacoue-

3. *New York Times*, 20 August 1993, 1(A), 6(B).
4. See Paul Cummins, *Dachau Song* (Peter Lang, 1993).

Labarthe told the following anecdote in a 1990 seminar. Discussing another form of music Lacoue-Labarthe himself both admires and plays, he described Miles Davis performing shortly before his death and stopping, midphrase, to utter an expletive. "He was working," Lacoue-Labarthe explained. In the caesura not of speech but of music, filling in with an empty word for a musical phrase he could not find, Miles shows how music is simultaneously inside the body, of the subject, and beyond.

Preface

Four "scenes" compose this book, all four made over Wagner, directly or indirectly: two by French poets (Baudelaire, Mallarmé), two others by German philosophers (Heidegger, Adorno). Obviously music is at issue, but also theater and even myth and a broad claim, clearly announced in the face of poetry, to making possible once again a "great art," a modern equivalent to tragedy, that is to say, to a properly religious art.

The stakes are thus also political.

The first two scenes, set in the last century, are contemporary with the European triumph of Wagnerism; they took place, whether during Wagner's lifetime or not, in a historical sequence punctuated by the Franco-Prussian War of 1870 and the Commune, where the worldwide unleashing of nations and classes was announced—and *prefigured*. The two others, in this century, took place when certain effects of Wagnerism, not only ideological, made themselves heard, and when the confusion of the "national" and the "social" seemed to solidify in a political *configuration* that was monstrously new. In both cases, art and politics are played together, but neither in the form of a politics of art nor, even less, in the form of an art of politics. It is a more serious matter, the matter of the *aestheticization*—the *figuration*—of the political.

These four scenes, all played at a distance, even the first (in 1865), frame in a certain way, and perhaps also help illuminate, the "true scene"—here left in the background—which sanctioned Nietzsche's rupture with Wagner, this assuredly major philosophical event about which Heidegger, despite the grudge we bear against him, was not completely wrong to say, in 1938, that it is crucial to understand it "as the necessary turning point of our history" (even if this possessive reinforced, at once maladroitly and scandalously, the very power of that with which Nietzsche wanted to break in breaking with Wagner).

The background of this study merits some explanation. It will serve here as an introduction.

~

First, there is the question of music, which, strangely, is never a question of music alone.

Since the end of the Renaissance—even since the time of Petrarch and the *Ars nova*, in any case since the appearance of the modern in the modern sense of the word—Western music (for three centuries at least) has been principally defined as *musica ficta* (I am guided here by Adorno's analyses). Even the school of Vienna, perhaps putting aside Webern, does not take issue with this determination. Let us admit, to simplify (as it is generally done), that this novelty was more or less limited to the art of song and that everything began with the invention of the *stile rappresentativo* and of what Monteverdi called the *seconda prattica*—which should also have been the revelatory title of a treaty (or manifesto) that was announced but never published: *The Second Practice or Perfection of Modern Music*. What did this discovery consist in?

Discovering, first of all, that is to say finding (again), what no discovery, in the sense of discovering a treasure, could give the hope of restoring: declamation in the antique manner, which one wanted to oppose, in the name of the modern, to the ecclesiastical norms of music, the *prima prattica* (polyphony and counterpoint) or the *musica perfecta*, as Palestrina had just illustrated it. Verdi's famous order, in reality only a technical suggestion, "Let us make progress by returning to the antique," could have an emblematic value here. (Likewise, although with an extra twist, this title of a 1555 treaty: *Antique Musique Reduced to Modern Practice*.) Modern ducted in the last years of the cinquecento is ordered, as is well known, by the dream of reestablishing tragedy. On the basis of a sort of *ut musica poesis*—also clearly thematized by Vecchi: "Music is poetry by the same right as poetry is music"—one sought a renaissance of what one imagined to have been a total art. (A "renaissance" of tragedy is also the key word of the propaganda of Bayreuth, as we see in *The Birth of Tragedy*.) From the *Camerata fiorentina*—the Academia Bardi—to Mantua and to Venice, in all of erudite Italy, an intense study of Aristotle's *Poetics* was undertaken, practically the only document that classical antiquity had left us on Athenian theater. It was translated and commentated, in an attempt, following the example of Vincènzo Galilei, to draw from it the principles and rules for a practice of *dramma per musica*, which was thus, by an obvious necessity, first an affair of music or musical invention. That is why the renaissance of tragedy, which is really the only birth of it that we know (this renaissance being a birth of something other than what tragedy had been, which remains forever lost), destined the new art, under the effect of a strange constraint, to represent by predilection the birth of music, and to "sing" its incomparable power. From the *Euridice* of Peri to the *Orfeo* of Monteverdi, in this first decade of the seventeenth century, opera was born as the celebration of the Western myth of music and lyricism. Or—this connection arises by itself— as the *figuration* of the metaphysical structure that is the very principle of the new art: the *Representation of Spirit and Body*, by Cavalieri, also dates from 1600. The initial *mise-en-abyme* of opera, as the modern genre par excellence: it would regularly reappear all during its history and would also finish by sealing its death or "closure" between *Moses and Aaron* and *Capriccio*. If the last word that philosophy pronounced on art—with which it also pronounced the end of art, at least so it thought—is that art is "the sensual presentation of a spiritual content," then *opera*, which not only emblematizes the famous conflict of *Prima la musica, dópo le parole* (or the reverse) but also mobilizes all the sensual apparatus capable of supporting an art, will have been the promise of the *oeuvre* as such (of the absolute *organon*, in the sense of Schelling):

genre itself, where art will be reengendered, for a time, but also where art—in the highest moments—will have reached its limit.

(This limit or extremity, we know, and I will return to it at length in the final chapter, is what is named, in a particular tradition, the "sublime." It must never be forgotten, when we think of the greatest of operas, that Kant suggested three modes of "presentation of the sublime" inasmuch as such a presentation, in his words, "applied to the Beaux-Arts": tragedy in verse, sacred oratorio, and the didactic or philosophical poem. Opera, ultimately, will have been found at the exact intersection between these three modes.)

It was Wagner, in the last century, who seized this promise of opera with both the greatest lucidity and instinctive force. (Which does not in any way exclude a certain artistic infantilism, a dubious penchant for mythology, or a surprising mix of metaphysical grandiloquence with an acuity for symbolic analysis or the allegorization of the historical world. But this is not important here: Wagner himself is not the object of this book, but rather the effect that he produced, which was immense.)

It is difficult today to form an idea of the shock that Wagner provoked, whether one admires him or scorns him. It was, all across Europe, an event; and if Wagnerism—a sort of mass phenomenon in the cultivated bourgeoisie—spread with this vigor and rapidity, it was due not only to the propagandizing talent of the master or to the zeal of his fanatics, but also to the sudden appearance of what the century had desperately tried to produce since the beginnings of romanticism—a work of "great art" on the scale imputed to works of Greek art, even the scale of great Christian art—here it was finally produced, and the secret of what Hegel had called the "religion of art" had been rediscovered. And de facto, what was founded was like a new religion.

To what could such an effect be due (other than to the need for religion, which, one hundred years ago, was not less than it is today)?

Essentially to two causes, which are closely linked.

The first is that opera, or musical drama, inasmuch as it saw it-self as the restitution of tragedy, owed its discovery and its rise only to the—obligatory—conversion of its native infirmity (the total ignorance of ancient music) into its strength: music, alone among the arts in having no model in antiquity, and thus the only art that one can effectively call modern, is the freest of the arts, and the most apt to realize, on a large scale, this *figuration* that is in es-sence written into its philosophical program.

The second is that no other art was capable of such power. Be-fore the invention of photography revealed, with the violence that is well known, the threat that hung over "the work of art in the age of mechanical reproduction," music, even more than painting or architecture—in any case in a much more spectacular manner—was the site of formidable technological innovations, which not only affected instrumentation but also all worked toward *amplifi-cation*. As the triumph of the symphony, among others, attested to; Mallarmé was not wrong on this point. Nietzsche noted one day, after he broke with Wagner, obviously, that one could date the be-ginning of the decline of opera (and of European music) from the overture of *Don Giovanni*: from the deployment of an enormous machinery of instruments and people to produce the effect of the beyond, and to incite terror. Yet with Wagner, musical amplifica-tion—and aesthetic accumulation—reached its peak, even though we have seen, or rather heard, better since. It even required a mu-tation, perhaps disastrous, in the art of singing, and a revision, at least glimpsed, of scenography in theaters with architecture "à l'italienne." Bayreuth is no doubt not the first artistic project con-ceived from the point of view of technology: their number since the Renaissance is legion. But it is the first to outlast, or at least seem to outlast, all other attempts to accede to greatness—from now on crushed by their abundance.

The truth is that the first mass art had just been born, through music (through technology).

It is there, of course, that we touch on the political or aesthetico-political problem.

~

Tragedy had been thought, in any case in the whole tradition of German idealism, to be the political art par excellence. That it had been, historically, a sort of political religion is not in doubt, but it acquired this reputation in the German dream of Greece—such that no other genre could seriously compete with it, whereas in France the obsession with the epic remained strong—essentially because it was understood as the ideal and unsurpassed presentation of the great mythic *figures*, with whom an assembled people could identify and thanks to whom its identity was properly constituted or organized. It is this figurative virtue and this "fictioning" power—an old image here again of *mimesis*—that assured its political efficacy, all the more so because the essence of art was confirmed in it in reality. In the sense, in any case, in which politics is where the destiny of peoples comes from; and we see clearly why in Europe in the last century or even in this one, and not only in Germany, the question was important.

A decisive trait of a certain German tradition issuing from romanticism—and of which the Third Reich, as I tried to show elsewhere under the title, precisely, of a "fiction of politics,"[1] is in many regards the accomplishment—is this belief in the necessity of a figure (a *Gestalt*) for the organization of the national community. It is in this sense that I risked the term "national aestheticism," which was perhaps not exclusively the territory of the German tradition, as we will see. In the philosophico-political discourse of the 1930's, in any case the one common to Jünger and Heidegger, for example, and to several others in the "revolutionary conservative" movement, such a figure is that of the Worker (and of the Soldier: the social and the national), even of the Führer. But we can well imagine that this haunting goes further back, to, among others, the romantic demand for a "new mythology" (but not only to this: it is also present in some ceremonials of the Enlightenment and of the French Revolution), and that it continues across the entire century—including the Nietzsche of *Zarathustra*—which has not ceased to be our provenance. Obviously, it does not spare Wagner, who made of it, definitively, his *entire* political program, which was, as we know, painfully detailed. One of the stakes of this book is to recall this, and to show that no aesthetic or artistic practice, for fundamental reasons that derive from the determination of the very essence of art, can declare itself politically innocent. This is not the "everything is political" of totalitarianism that destines art to be political. This is art itself, since it has been defined as such, in its highest ambition.

This is the guiding thread, or the *Leitmotiv*, that I wanted to follow here, trying to trace it across these four texts, which, two by two, and not by chance, define national adherence. But these four "stations" are not only destined to try to elucidate the general question of the figure and the fiction, or to measure their political stakes. In their very succession (each presenting in turn a lost recognition, a reticent rivalry, a declared hostility, but against the background of an analogous goal, the hope of a deliverance), they organize a sort of story or tale that, after the fact, I realize is not without analogy to the story of my own relationship to Wagner. A matter of *katharsis*, perhaps.

The four "scenes" are thus four studies, centered on the same questions and topic that have just been addressed, but nonetheless relatively independent in provenance or occasion. The first two were sketched in a seminar at the University of Montreal on "Music and the Theory of the Text," organized in 1980 by Christie MacDonald. A first version of the Baudelaire chapter was published under the title "Baudelaire contra Wagner" in *Etudes Françaises*, 17, nos. 3–4 (1982). The notes that served as a basis for a series of three discussions of Mallarmé were published as such in the journal *Recueil*, no. 4/5 (Champ Vallon, 1986), under the title "La musique à la lettre" (which would also have been one of the possible titles of this book).

The chapter on Heidegger, in a first version, was the object of a lecture at the seminar on philosophy directed by Lucien Braun at the University of Strasbourg in 1986. In this first version, it was published in the *Cahiers du Séminaire de philosophie* ("Musique et philosophie," P.U.S., 1987).

The essay on Schönberg and Adorno originated in a seminar

held at Berkeley in 1987 on the sublime. Condensed a first time into a lecture at the colloquium "L'Écriture du temps," organized by Marie-Louise Mallet in 1988 at Lyon under the aegis of the International College of Philosophy, it was reworked for a collective publication entitled *Opera Through Other Eyes* (Stanford University Press, 1993). A part of it was published by the journal *Détail*, no. 3/4 (Winter 1991), directed by Pierre Alféri and Suzanne Doppelt. Another was delivered at the colloquium "Art and the Sacred," organized in June 1990 in Strasbourg by Jean-Jacques Nillès for the International College of Philosophy.

My thanks go to all those who are responsible for these circumstances and publications.

MUSICA FICTA
(Figures of Wagner)

§1 Baudelaire

Music hollows out the heavens.

—Baudelaire

Who is he among us who has not, in his ambitious days,
dreamed of the miracle of a poetic prose, musical without
rhythm and without rhyme, supple and rough enough to
adapt itself to the lyric movements of the soul, to the undula-
tions of reverie, to the sudden starts of consciousness?

—Baudelaire

Everything begins with a letter.

One that Baudelaire addressed to Wagner on the 17th of Febru-
ary 1860, several days after the last of Wagner's three concerts at the
Théâtre des Italiens, during which he conducted some "excerpts"
from his works—*The Flying Dutchman*, *Tannhäuser*, *Lohengrin*,
and *Tristan*—apparently in order to prepare the way for his entrée
at the Paris Opéra. Subjugated by these works, Baudelaire decrees
them "sublime." To Poulet-Malassis he confides: "It was an event
that changed my thinking."[1] Angered by the attitude of the French
audience, he chooses to declare this to Wagner himself.

Here then, to begin, is the letter. There are few testimonials of
this kind of *recognition*:[2]

Sir,
    I've always imagined that however used to glory an artist might be,
he would not remain unmoved by a sincere compliment, when that
compliment resembled a cry of thanks. I believe, too, that this cry
could have special value coming from a Frenchman, that's to say,
from a man poorly suited to outbursts of enthusiasm and born in a
country where there is almost as little understanding of painting and
poetry as there is of music. Above all, I want to say that I am indebted
to you for *the greatest musical pleasure I've ever experienced*. I've reached
an age where one hardly enjoys writing to famous men anymore, and
I would have hesitated much longer to express my admiration to you

1

through a letter had I not day after day set eyes on unworthy, ridiculous articles in which all possible efforts are made to defame your
glory. Yours is not the first case where my country has caused me suffering and shame. In short, it's indignation that has led me to express
my gratitude. I said to myself: "I want to be distinguished from all
those jackasses."

The first time I went to the theater to hear your works I was pretty
ill-disposed toward them. I admit I even had a lot of bad prejudices.
But I had an excuse, for I've so often been a dupe. I've heard so much
music by charlatans making great claims. By you, I was instantly won
over. What I felt is beyond description, but if you'll deign not to
laugh, I'll try to convey my feelings to you. At first it seemed to me
that I knew this music already, and later, in thinking it over, I understood what had caused this illusion. It seemed to me that the music
was *my own*, and I recognized it as any man recognizes those things he
is destined to love. For anyone who isn't a man of intelligence such a
claim would seem ridiculous in the extreme, above all when it's written by someone who, like me, *does not know music* and whose entire
musical education extends no further than having heard (admittedly
with great gratification) a few fine pieces by Weber and by Beethoven.

Then the element that struck me above all was the grandeur of
your music. It represents the heights, and it drives the listener on to
the heights. In all your works, I've found the solemnity of Nature's
great sounds, her great aspects, and the solemnity, too, of the great
human passions. One instantly feels swept up and subjugated. One of
the strangest pieces, one of those that aroused in me a new musical
emotion, is that designed to depict religious ecstasy. The effect produced by "The Introduction of the Guests" and "The Marriage Feast"
is immense. I felt all the majesty of a life greater than the one we lead.
And another thing, too: in hearing it, I frequently experienced a rather
odd emotion, which could be described as the pride and the pleasure
[*jouissance*] of comprehension, of allowing myself to be penetrated
and invaded—a truly sensual pleasure, recalling that of floating
through the air or rolling on the sea. And at the same time the music
occasionally expressed all the pride of life. Generally those deep har-
monies seemed to me comparable to those stimulants that speed up
the pulse of the imagination. Finally, I experienced in addition—and
I beg you not to laugh—feelings that probably stem from my particular cast of mind and my frequent preoccupations. Your music is full

of something that is both uplifted and uplifting, something that longs to climb higher, something excessive and superlative. To illustrate this, let me use a comparison borrowed from painting. I imagine a vast extent of red spreading before my eyes. If this red represents passion, I see it change gradually, through all the shades of red and pink, until it reaches the incandescence of a furnace. It would seem difficult, even impossible, to render something more intensely hot, and yet a final flash traces a whiter furrow on the white that provides its background. That, if you will, is the final cry of a soul that has soared to a paroxysm of ecstasy.

I had begun to write a few meditations on the pieces from *Tannhäuser* and *Lohengrin* that we heard, but I recognized the impossibility of saying it all.

I could thus continue this letter interminably. If you've been able to read this, accept my thanks. I've been repeating to myself over and over again, particularly in hours of despondency: "If only I could hear some Wagner tonight!" No doubt there are others like me. All in all you must have been satisfied with the general audience, whose instincts were far above the poor science of the journalists. Why don't you give some more concerts, adding new pieces? You've given us a foretaste of new joys; do you have the right to deprive us of the rest? Once more, sir, my thanks. You recalled me to myself and to what is great, in bad times.

Ch. Baudelaire

I am not including my address, for that might make you think I had something to ask of you.[3]

Putting aside for the moment an examination of this text, I will point out only the strange negative or aborted promise Baudelaire makes to Wagner, from one great artist to another ("I had begun to write a few meditations") in the purest form of renunciation ("but I recognized the impossibility of saying it all"). He adds, "I could thus continue this letter interminably." The letter is therefore only a letter because it virtually contains a text—poetic or critical, the word "meditation" barely allows us to decide—a text that the letter is only a part of, or that it outlines. But, we must understand, Wagner's music, and the *jouissance* that it is able to create, are so great that the task of writing about it is revealed as being interminable and thus impossible. The message is clear: music infinitely overwhelms the possibilities of writing. And this is very clearly the first message that Baudelaire addresses to Wagner, the most immediate form of his "recognition": the *power* of music is infinite. Yet barely two months later, Baudelaire's decision is made: he will write a "great work" on Wagner, and even if he never stops complaining, as usual, of this so-called "grand travail," the following year he will publish *Richard Wagner and "Tannhäuser" in Paris*, probably written at the last minute—"improvised in three days" he says to his mother, in his "obsession with print"—but all the same "meditated" on for some months.

This essay, it is generally agreed, is Baudelaire's last great critical or "theoretical" text, the measure of the last great "aesthetic" *shock* that Wagner's music represented for him. But the type of shock, and its almost immediate translation into the letter, even its declaration of powerlessness, served more than sufficiently to communicate it. Why then did Baudelaire again take up the "work," particularly so doggedly, as nearly all of the documentation suggests? In order to confirm to Wagner the truth of his letter and of his "recognition"? Because, in one way or another, he might have felt indebted to Wagner? In order to make up for the affront in effect constituted by the attitude of the French audience? No doubt. All of these reasons, and others, are clearly part of it. But it is not impossible to imagine another one, more essential, one that, perhaps, alone might explain the enormous work Baudelaire engaged in for an entire year, the last year of his life that was actually productive.

By 1860, Baudelaire had written almost all of what he had to write. This is true, at any rate, of his critical essays. In other words, by this date, Baudelaire's aesthetic is completely constituted. The question is then: what constrains Baudelaire, one last time, to begin digging again? The "event" of Wagner's music, certainly. And at any rate, he says so himself. But we remark rather quickly that this event is first of all simply a musical one: "having heard (admittedly with great gratification) a few fine pieces by Weber and by Beethoven" is not entirely the same thing as experiencing this *jouissance* he declares as being without equal. In reality, what is happening here is that, for someone who had constructed his whole aesthetic on painting and poetry (or in a wider sense, literature), this is the revelation of music itself. There were, here and there in the poems, allusions to music or certain musicians, and even something that could easily be identified as a "thematics" of music, which nevertheless remains vague. There was also, more muffled, but detectable—Baudelaire's successors, beginning with Verlaine, will not mistake it—a true "musical haunting,"[4] inherited from Nerval, perhaps, or from Hoffmann, which, beyond any consideration of the musicality of his language, could make us think that the goal secretly aimed at by this poetry was ultimately a kind of music. But nothing, at any rate, that had ever constrained Baudelaire to examine the question specifically. Why then does this revelation make it necessary?

The immediate response is the one that Baudelaire himself formulates in advance; in substance: this music was mine, I recognized it, I must explain this. Undoubtedly; and I will return to this motif, which is, in fact, essential. But this evidence need not conceal another movement, less perceptible, it is true, but all the same marked enough to call for a second answer: it is that, for the first time, Baudelaire is really confronted with an art that threatens the long-affirmed supremacy of poetry. That is to say, of *his* art. This is the underlying threat within the *recognition*, in all its meanings, declared in the letter. And this is what the important essay of 1861 attempts to exorcise by any means.

What is it that constitutes this threat?

〜

Even if Baudelaire had not read *Opera and Drama*, which is what he leaves us to believe (it is true that he mentions only having "procured" the English translation published as a review several years earlier), it is certain on the other hand that he had read, and read closely, the "Letter on Music," which was written by Wagner in 1860 as a special introduction to the French publication of *Four Poems for Opera*[5] and in which Wagner effectively organizes and condenses the principal themes of *Opera and Drama*. Baudelaire, in other words, has not only undergone the shock of this music, or of music per se; he has also directly confronted Wagner's theoretical writing, and when he speaks of his "work" during the year in which he develops his essay, he is first of all thinking of this reading of Wagner and of several other related readings, of Liszt, for example. He must assimilate, all at once, a theoretical construction for which nothing had prepared him beforehand (Baudelaire knows very little about the German realm) and which is all the more imposing or formidable in that it brings with it a whole philosophical tradition about which he knows nothing, or very little: through De Quincey, he had just caught a few echoes of Coleridge and the "German metaphysics"; but he has nothing but scorn for "Hegelianism," and apparently Schopenhauer's name is unknown to him. Moreover, it must not be forgotten that, despite Nerval, and despite Madame de Staël's popularization of the themes of the romanticism of Jena, France in general is at this time living in ignorance of what speculative idealism had produced as regards art theory. French romanticism, though it figures in European romanticism, has barely any relation except with the second German romanticism—Hoffmann, for example; and if one can in fact consider Baudelaire the first French writer to recover something of the original philosophical inspiration of romanticism, it must be attributed to his own genius, and not to his knowledge of the theories. But with Wagner, he is directly in the line of fire, hit by a *theory*, in the strongest sense of the term, that certainly has neither the metaphysical depth nor the systematic rigor of the great German idealism from which it borrows, but that nevertheless does not lack coherence, or, if read with Schopenhauer in mind, metaphysical ambition. To tell the truth, it is from Wagner's arrival on the French stage that, at least in the matter of aesthetics, the arrival in France of German metaphysics and the divulgence of speculative romanticism's fundamental theses must be dated. And it is Baudelaire who first experiences its *shock*.

It is necessary to speak of *shock* a second time here, because underlying the musical revelation there is another revelation, difficult to accept and even scandalous, which is that if Wagner's music attains such power, it does so in the exact measure to which it proceeds with the express and deliberate will to supplant, if not to finish, poetry. Wagner's arrival is, from this point of view, an intrusion. It represents an attack on and disruption of the "beaux-arts system" that more or less explicitly regulates French aesthetics and that is in essence, despite Rousseau and despite Berlioz, a writer's aesthetic, concerned with preserving the primacy of poetry and completely occupied with adapting itself to the recent concept of *literature.* Yet the issue that Wagner reopens and whose trial he begins with such tumult, a half century after Jena, is precisely the issue of literature.

This, then, is a first sign. The work of art, as Wagner understands and propounds it, represents a double challenge: first to "literature" itself, the concept of which, in the process of sedimentation, already implies that it is essentially a story, or narrative fiction, and that it is consequently completed in the modern age in the genre beyond all genres, the novel. (Wagner, by choosing the theater and drama, or by invoking Greek tragedy, is thoroughly contesting the "progressivism" of literary theory.) But it also represents a challenge to poetry, more narrowly defined, which it puts in competition with music, reversing, following Schopenhauer's rather simple logic, the (logocentrist) metaphysical hierarchy of the arts, as it is established in Hegel's *Aesthetics,* for example. And we know that this reversal also bears the stamp of dialectical operativity itself, as will be the case again in *The Birth of Tragedy*: what is already beginning to be translated as "the total work of art," the *Gesamtkunstwerk*—which is the Work in absolute terms, the absolute *organon* of Schelling, or, as Nietzsche will say, the *opus metaphysicum*—posits itself as the very *end* of art in the form of the unification and synthesis (this is the word Wagner uses) of all the individual arts. Such a synthesis is in sum the accomplishing or achieving of *mousikè*, in its Greek meaning. This is the reason why this synthesis is given the right, in its modern translation, to be made into the *musical* sublation of all the arts, and above all of the signifying art par excellence, the one that the whole tradition, or nearly, has described envying because it is granted as having the greatest power of exposition or presentation, the *Darstellung*: the art of language, poetry in its broadest sense, which is literature it-self, or what the Germans will for a long time, authorized by ro-manticism, call *Dichtung*. In this sense, Wagner reopens the ques-tion of literature because he reopens, on bases relatively new in re-gard to the preceding century, despite Diderot and Rousseau, the debate or combat, the *agôn*, between music and poetry.

This already goes quite far in explaining Baudelaire's surprising reaction, but it is not all. Underneath the imperious, very visible gesture of the musician is hidden a more suspicious one, which touches even more deeply the question of literature. Because what Wagner is in reality concerned with, when he subjugates poetry, is the genre in which the moderns, since the romantics, have seen the secret essence of literature or *Dichtung* in its *subjective* defini-tion; that is, in *lyricism*. And that is where Baudelaire is hit.

We know that on the model of French poetics of the eighteenth century, for example that of Batteux, romanticism and idealism interpret the Platonic tripartition of the modes of *lexis* or of enun-ciation as a distribution of fundamental genres, that they index by the opposition of subjective and objective. It is thus that simple diegesis is identified with lyricism, that is, with the subjective genre; that the mimetic mode is identified with the genre of drama, itself decreed as being objective; and that mixed enuncia-tion, which for Plato refers back to the epic, ends up by designat-ing the subjective-objective genre of the novel, which brings about the dialectical sublation of the two others.[6] This is exactly why the novel finishes literature—when literature is not, as for the Schle-gels, criticism itself, which poses a completely different problem. However, in that lyricism is rightly or wrongly considered the most primitive genre, that is, the most spontaneous, and in that litera-ture and art in general, whether it be the worked-on or the work-ing, are overdetermined by the concept of the subject (such that the sublation of arts or of genres always happens in the direction of the subjective), lyricism remains the germinal seed of all literature and, probably, its purest modality. We see this very clearly in Bau-delaire, who ceaselessly turns the novel, Balzac's for example, and its supposed realism (or its supposed objectivity) back into an absolutely speculative genre, even if the price he pays for this is the theory of genius and of the sublime.[7] In romanticism, in spite of everything—in spite of the "theory of the novel"—lyricism remains the stakes of literature in its essence. Against which Wagner opposes, as its truth, music. That is to say, if we can play on this distinction, a *lyric*.

Reading Baudelaire's essay closely, we notice immediately that he has essentially preserved four theorems from the "Letter on Music."

The first appears during a long argument devoted to the state and the progress of the arts in Europe, considered from the point of view of their relation to languages. A Fichtean argument, it could be said, or more generally a romantic one, but one that in reality derives from Herder:[8] the *formal* superiority of Italian, French, and Spanish arts is explained by these nations' belonging to the area of Romance languages. In comparison to these nations, with their perfection of "Latin" art since the Renaissance, the German nation is inferior and lags behind, having been both artistically and culturally "colonized." Hence the German reaction, not destined to revive a "stifled . . . German form" (such a *form* does not exist) but to reflect on form itself in general and the conditions of the possibility of its universalization. This is why, Wagner says, German art as such begins, with Goethe and Schiller, when it converts its inferiority into an advantage, and especially when it comes directly face to face with authentic Greek art (not filtered through Romanness) in order to promote an *ideal form*, "purely human," that is to say in fact "supranational."[9]

According to Wagner, only music could claim to produce this universal and ideal form, and of course the whole problem of musical "significance"[10] is here in play:

> If, as to literature, the diversity of European languages creates an obstacle to this universality, music is one language that is equally intelligible to all men, and it should be the conciliating power, the sovereign language, which, resolving ideas into feelings, offers a universal organ of the most private aspect of the artist's intuition: an organ with a limitless capacity, above all if the plastic expression of theatrical rep-

resentation gives it this light that painting alone has until now claimed as its exclusive privilege. (pp. 27–28)

We see it here: what music as a universal form, a "language equally intelligible to all men," is put in competition with is, namely, *literature*, which is linked—and subordinated—to the diversity of natural languages. All literature is personal, and, it must be believed, so is all thought because the mind, unlike feeling, which rebels against language, has no possibility of freeing itself from language. If music, on the other hand, is posited as a universal, this is because it is—Rousseau's legacy—essentially *dynamic* and thus capable of adequately translating, even immediately expressing, the intensity of feelings. It is known that the most spontaneous expression of passion or, as Hegel said, even of subjective interiority is singing. But because it is thus conceived as a form with *dunamis*, as a form-power or a form-force, music possesses the power to act and to *operate*. In other words, music *works*, in the dialectic sense of the word: it has the power to *conciliate*, to unify different forms, and that is why it dominates, why it is "sovereign"; but it also has the power to *resolve* (this is the *Auflösung* of speculative logic), that is to say to *sublate* the mind—which is enslaved to language—in and through feeling, and that is why it provides the "universal organ."

This *operation* has only one goal, that of accomplishing the *subjective* determination of art and the artwork, in conformity with the romantic program. But differing from what happens in speculative romantic philosophy, the "synthesis" happens not according to the mind but according to feeling. And consequently, from the point of view of creation itself, according to the "intuition" of the artist—of the subject of the work. Thus the paradox of art that serves as the basis for Wagner's argument, and that is ruled by what I have elsewhere attempted to define as the mimetic logic (*mime-tologic*)[11] in Diderot and Hölderlin: the "universal organ" is in fact the organ "of the most private aspect of the artist's intuition." In other words, the more subjective it is, the more objective it is (that is the reason why it takes a theater, a structure of *mimesis*, for such an *organon*, which Wagner, here at least, compromises a little naively with the necessity of adding the "plastic."[12] Or, if one prefers: the more music expresses or signifies what is purely subjective, the pure depths of singular intuition, the more it is in a position to speak of the universal, the "purely human." Which literature, or more generally, language, cannot do inasmuch as it already claims a certain universality that prevents it from returning to pure subjective interiority. That is why literature cannot, in any way, accede to the rank of the *art of the subject*: language prevents the subject from overtaking or reappropriating itself. There is only one means of subjective appropriation, and that is music.[13]

The second of the theories held by Baudelaire is part of an argument devoted to the decomposition of Greek tragedy, to the "dispersion" of the arts (to their separation, owing to the fact that art is no longer the "teacher and spiritual guide for public life"— again, a political theme), and consequently to the disappearance of the specific power originally attached to art. The project of reconstructing a "total art," "the art work of the future," takes root in such an account (concurrent with Baudelaire's reference to a "poetry of the future"), whose principle Wagner here summarizes:

> Armed with the authority of the most eminent critics, for example, with the research of a Lessing on the limits of painting and poetry, I believed myself in possession of a solid result: it is that each art tends toward an indefinite extension of its power, that this tendency leads it finally to its limit, and that it would not know how to pass this limit without running the risk of losing itself in the incomprehensible, the bizarre, and the absurd. Arriving there, I seemed to see clearly that each art demands, as soon as it reaches the limits of its power, to give a hand to the neighboring art; and in view of my ideal, I found a lively interest in following this tendency in each individual art: it seemed to me that I could demonstrate it in the most striking manner in the relations between poetry and music, above all in the presence of the extraordinary importance that modern music has achieved. I was thus seeking to represent to myself the work of art that must embrace all the individual arts and make them cooperate in the superior realization of its object; I arrived in this way at the meditated conception of the ideal that had obscurely been formed in me, a vague image to which the artist aspired. (pp. 38–39)

Everything rests, then, on the refusal of the transgression: each art, because it "tends toward an indefinite extension of its power," is ordered by a sort of law of the "passage to the limit": but if it tries to move beyond this limit, and this will be exactly the enterprise of modern art (Wagner sees things very clearly), it is threatened with absurdity or inanity.

The dialectical confrontation of the individual arts in the "total work of art" is consequently a means of containing excess and safeguarding meaning. It is, like all dialectical operations, a strictly economic measure. The totalizing gesture is a gesture of closure—which, in Wagner's case, is obviously aggravated by the "Restoration" or even the "revolutionary-conservative" aspect. And as once again the relationship between the arts focuses on the relation between music and poetry, we see without difficulty—and this will be confirmed later by the role that Wagner has "infinite melody" play in this operation—that the overflow that is to be contained here is the overflow of poetry. Poetry, in its very tendency toward excess, in its power of transgression, represents in fact the greatest threat. Mallarmé will be very sensitive to this; but before him, it is an argument that will not have left Baudelaire indifferent.

He encountered it in a third passage where, taking up the analysis set forth in *Opera and Drama*, Wagner asks himself why great poets have tried to make themselves into great opera librettists, thus manifesting their "desires . . . to see opera raised to the heights of an ideal genre." It is apparent that Wagner is thinking of Goethe, who as we know had dreamed of writing a sequel to *The Magic Flute*:

> I was seeking the meaning of these obstinate hopes; I found its explanation, it seemed to me, in a natural penchant of the poet that dominates the conception as well as the form of his work: this penchant is to employ the instrument of abstract ideas, language, in such a way that it acts on sensibility itself. This tendency is manifest in the invention of the poetic subject; the only tableau of human life that is called poetic is that where motifs, which have no sense but for abstract intelligence, give way to the purely human movements that govern the heart. The same tendency is the sovereign law that presides

over poetic form and representation. The poet seeks, in his language, to substitute for the abstract and conventional value of words their sensitive and original signification; the rhythmic arrangement and ornament (already nearly musical) of rhyme are the means of assuring for verse, for the sentence, a power that captivates as if by a spell, and governs feeling at its will. Essential to the poet, this tendency leads him up to the limit of his art, a limit that music immediately touches; and consequently the most complete work of the poet ought to be the one that, in its final achievement, would be a perfect music. (pp. 45–46)

The metaphysics of the language at work here is still the same: it is basically Rousseauist. It belongs to what Derrida, in *Of Grammatology*, identified as "the age of Rousseau." It rests on the simple opposition—itself overdetermined by the opposition between the intelligible and the perceptible—between, on the one hand, speech or language, the instrument of abstract ideas, and, on the other hand, music as the expression of feeling. And it does so twice: with respect to the content (the poetic "subject"), but also with respect to form, to the mode of exposition or presentation. As to *Darstellung*. Poetry is a use of language destined to give to language what language itself cannot give, neither in expression nor in the effect it has produced or will produce, which is not beyond but on this side of intellectual or rhetorical effect, an effect of enchantment and fascination: "A power," says Wagner, "that captivates as if by a spell."

Of course this conception of poetry can without difficulty invoke poets' own discourse on poetry: the romantic and postromantic arguments on the "magic of words," including the "evocative sorcery" of Baudelaire himself, are not taken into account. Poetry, in other words, supplies music with arms, simply because it shares, with regard to language, the same metaphysical presuppositions. When Wagner announces that poetry is in sum a protomusic, signaled by its rhythm or rhyme (elsewhere he will say more about assonance and alliteration, which he himself uses often), he is only repeating contemporary dogma. Yet he moves beyond dogma when he draws out its ultimate consequences in a *systematic* way; that is to say, when drawing the argument from the law of passage to the limit, he affirms that "the most complete work of the poet should be the one that, in its final achievement, would be a perfect music." Completion, achievement—this is the lexicon of totalization. We will agree that something entirely different from the simple collaboration of arts "working together" is outlined here.

What remains is to understand what gives music its incomparable power. This is where the last theorem comes in. To produce it, Wagner recapitulates at some length the history of music and its modern "perfecting." This culminates, naturally, in German music since Hayden, that is to say, in Beethoven, whose work effects the "synthesis" of the "primitive rhythmic melody" of the dance or orchestral music of the Greeks and the harmony of Christian music (Palestrina, the Protestant chorale) in what Wagner calls "melodic expression." (Melody is always presented as the sublation of the opposition between rhythm and harmony: this is the basis of Wagnerian "melocentrism.")

The model of this *achieved* music is the Beethoven symphony, which carries musical "language" to unheard of heights:

In this symphony the instruments speak a language of which no previous age had any knowledge; because the expression, purely musical even in its nuances of the most astonishing diversity, captivates the listener for a duration unheard of until then, moves his soul with an energy that no other art can attain; it reveals to him in its variety a regularity so free and so bold that its power necessarily surpasses for us all logic, even when the laws of logic are not at all contained in it, and that, on the contrary, rational thought, which proceeds by principle and consequence, finds no foothold here. The symphony must then appear to us, in the most rigorous sense, as the revelation of another world; in the fact, it unveils for us a series of phenomena of the world that differs absolutely from the logical habitual series; and the series that it reveals to us presents first of all an incontestable character: it is to impose itself on us with the most irresistible persuasion, and to govern our feelings with an empire so absolute that it confounds and fully disarms logical reason. (pp. 56–57)

This is Schopenhauer, scarcely paraphrased: music is the revelation, the epiphany, of metaphysics itself. (Nietzsche, himself taking up Schopenhauer's terminology in *The Birth of Tragedy*, will translate it thus: the immediate duplication of an originary One, which is will.) But for Wagner, on this point closer to Herder than to Schopenhauer,[14] such a revelation is *historic*. It has become the task of modern music—that is, German music, liberated thanks to Luther from Roman music (or Romanesque, in both the imperial and ecclesiastical meanings of the term)—to open up the possibility of a new and probably definitive ontological revelation: the being of what is is will; the essence of man is the heart (feeling), not reason. Through this "metaphysical necessity," as Wagner himself calls it, music has become the most powerful language there is, all the more powerful in having arisen upon the "more and more conventional perfecting of the modern idioms," that is, upon the degradation or disappearance, itself historic (this is the whole question of "progress"), of the primitive motivation of the sign. Or for Wagner, of the word.[15]

Under these conditions, what task remains for poetry?

Here is the reply:

> In the presence of this novelty that it would be impossible not to recognize, there remained henceforth for poetry only two ways to develop: it was necessary for it to pass in a complete manner into the field of abstraction, of the pure combination of ideas, of the representation of the world by means of the logical laws of thought: however, this work is that of philosophy and not of poetry; or rather it needed to meld intimately with music and with the music whose infinite power the Beethoven symphony revealed.
>
> Poetry will find the means for this without difficulty; it will recognize that its secret and profound inspiration is finally to resolve itself in music, as soon as it perceives in music a need that, in its turn, only poetry can satisfy. (pp. 59–60)

The alternative is thus very simple. Either poetry stays in its element, language and nothing more, and becomes philosophy, *disappears* like philosophy, which inverts the most explicit romantic-speculative program, Schelling's for example, and which will be addressed by the Nietzsche of *Zarathustra* (Nietzsche after the rupture with Wagner), who wants philosophy to reach its end, flow back to its original source, poetry, through the invention of a "new mythology."[16] Or else poetry must dissolve, "resolve" itself, in music—which is not the same as being threatened a second time with disappearance, but which on the contrary represents its only hope for survival. This is also why Wagner imagines this musical resolution of poetry as a kind of chemical process (on this point again, the Wagnerian dialectic is more romantic than properly Hegelian): it is, he says a few pages further, "an equal and reciprocal penetration of music and poetry" (p. 69).

What then should poetry do? It will in fact assume the task of articulating a response to the philosophical question that music inevitably poses, like every other important world phenomenon, but a question that music itself, because of its inability to *articulate* it, is unable to answer. It will consequently assume the task of answering the *metaphysical* question par excellence, which is of course the question "Why?" But it will never discharge this task except on the condition—it is an *abandon*, in every sense—of letting the poem "penetrate into the most minute fibers of musical tissue . . . in such a way that the idea that it expresses is entirely resolved in feeling" (and it is clearly still the same chemical or chemical-physiological metaphor when it is not, as can be found in many examples, openly sexual). This means for Wagner: the only poetry possible from now on is dramatic-musical poetry—formerly the opera "libretto"—inasmuch as it will have the function of presenting the idea in a perceptible way (the Hegelian definition of art), that is to say, the idea as myth (the romantic utopia of art). A little earlier, Wagner had said:

> From there, I saw myself necessarily led to designate *myth* as the poet's ideal matter. Myth is the primitive and anonymous poem of the people, and we find it in every age taken up, redone again ceaselessly by the great poets of cultivated periods. In myth, in fact, human relations nearly completely strip off their conventional form, which is intelligible only to abstract reason; they show what life has of the truly human, of the eternally comprehensible, and show it in this concrete

form, exclusive of all imitation, which gives to all true myths their individual character, which you recognize at the first glance. (p. 46)

The "poetry of the future," therefore, is myth. This is what Wagner teaches Baudelaire. However, myth is something different from a *poncif*, a pattern.[17]

It is different from a *poncif* because the *political* stakes, here, are immense. We know that the political positions and itineraries of Baudelaire and Wagner from 1848 on are not without analogy. Theirs is a story, from then on a classic, of revolutionary disappointment. But this analogy remains superficial, even if we rightly remark that in neither case did the ideological palinode erase or attenuate the earlier "radicalism." It is well known that radicalism (almost) always leads to palinode, that is, a return to the unknown truth of the original position. And if we register a certain anti-Semitism in both cases, we would not be allowing ourselves to be mistaken by appearances.[18] The terrain on which Wagner builds his *aesthetic* politics—the final trait with a false similarity to Baudelaire—is of an entirely different nature from the terrain familiar to French artists of the same era. (This is moreover why Wagner is a political man, unlike Baudelaire, and why his art theory will have considerable ideological influence.)

Wagner's aesthetic politics has nothing of a political aestheticism or of an "aesthete" politics (which will yet be the case with Baudelaire): rather it aims at what Benjamin and Brecht, speaking of Nazism, called an *aestheticization of politics*. This makes for an entirely different program. I attempted to show elsewhere, in the case of Heidegger,[19] that a certain German tradition, issuing from romanticism and from idealism, makes of art not just *a* political stake, but *the* political stake itself. Wagner belongs by right to this tradition; he is even its most important—let's say "fin-de-siècle"— representative, and it is he who, by this title, authorizes the ideological arguments of the "imperial" and then "revolutionary-conservative" style, of what Langbehn will end up naming with the *mot juste* "Kunstpolitik." Fritz Stern is right in calling this a term that designates not a politics of art but an aestheticized politics:[20] the assumption of the political as a work of art.

The essential is derived from this: that art recover its mythic capacity; what it recovers is its agogic capacity. Myth, defined as "the primitive and anonymous poem of the people"—it is a topos of middle romanticism—is thought of in the modern age (that is to say the age of de-Christianization) as the only *means of identification* that authorizes the fitting recognition of a nation experiencing birth pains such as those of the improbable Germany. The German political question that had not ceased, since the French Revolution and Napoleon (that is, let us say, since Fichte), to burden European politics is the question of national identity or, to use speculative terms, of the constitution of a people-subject. It is a matter of the appearance of the spirit of a people. It implies in this name a specific strategy that is in reality nothing other than the strategy of *Kulturkampf,* if we understand by that the struggle led against European "civilization," that is to say neoclassical culture, in view of a more original appropriation of the Greek model and of the institution, according to the purest of the agonistic logics, of a great German art, imagined as being the only one capable, in imitation of the Homeric epic or the Athenian tragedy, of defining the German being. The period from Lessing and Winckelmann to Nietzsche—and even well beyond: up to the Heidegger of the 1930's, and all during the era of national socialism—is haunted by the German "aestheticized politics." We should think of the watchword used by Nietzsche when preparing *Zarathustra*: "To build the myth of the future." Everything is contained therein, regardless of Nietzsche's *probity* concerning German politics elsewhere.

The Wagnerian project—it will soon be Bayreuth—is indissociable from this politics. Baudelaire probably does not guess this (whereas Mallarmé, after 1870, will be very conscious of it); nevertheless it is to this that he feels obliged to respond.

∾

And faced with this program, what is Baudelaire's reaction?

As surprising as it may seem, it is disarmingly simple: he is subjugated, he acquiesces, he submits. And even more surprising, it is not only this discourse that he accepts, that is to say this "theorization." He also accepts its whole presupposition; he accepts and recognizes the terrain itself on which the discourse is founded and on which the work is built. Which, first of all, is equal to saying: he accepts, without the least reserve, the absolute primacy of subjectivity.

This is the reason why, in the first place, Baudelaire reacts as a *subject*. The clearest form of submission is to say "I," to speak in the first person, in his own name.

Because this is how Baudelaire's important 1861 essay opens: on a reclamation of the "I," of the first person, which goes far beyond a personal investment or the reclamation of critical responsibility. If there is a reclamation, it is made in reality under the false modesty of the remark, in the name of *literature* as Baudelaire conceives of it, that is to say in the name of the subjectivity of him who wants to be indissociably poet (writer) and critic, and whose task will be precisely, confronted with the work of Wagner, to "recount his own impressions":

> Pray let us go back thirteen months, to the time when the whole affair began; and may I, in the course of the following appreciation, be allowed to speak often in my own name. That "I," justly taxed with impertinence in many cases, implies, however, a high degree of modesty; it imprisons the writer within the strictest limits of sincerity. By reducing the extent of his task, it makes it easier for him. And finally, there is no need to be a great expert in probabilism to acquire the conviction that this sincerity will win friends amongst impartial readers; the chances evidently are that even the ingenuous critic, in recording his own impressions, will also be recording those of some unknown supporters.[21]

Yet the "I"—the subject—who is involved here, and who comes to answer for Wagner in order to respond simultaneously to Wagner and to his detractors, is not the subject of a rhetorical artifice or facility; it is rather a subject who, up to a certain point, asks *himself* about Wagner, that is to say, expects from Wagnerian art, essentially from his music (this is practically all he knew of Wagner), that the music constitute him as such, that it return his own image to him, that it give him the opportunity to appropriate or to reappropriate himself. It is a subject who expects from Wagner's music, or recognizes in this music, his *means of identification*.

This is what the letter had said very clearly a few months earlier. In it, without circumlocution, Baudelaire had mentioned his submission and his subjugation (this is his word)—his demand, we might say today. An ideal demand, of course, as the end of his letter indicates, just after the decisive sentence ("You recalled me to myself"), the postscript *I have nothing to ask of you*, which is every-thing one could want short of a disclaimer. Baudelaire here has absolutely nothing to ask for: he asks *himself*; he wonders; and wondering is precisely asking nothing, or asking for what one knows one will never obtain because it would be a gift preceding all demand and even preceding any possibility of receiving: the gift of what by right remains inaccessible to oneself. The gift of be-ing oneself.

But before being the opportunity for such a "metaphysical" stake, Baudelaire's demand—it is worth underlining—is double. It is first of all (presented as) personal—you have conquered me de-spite my initial reticence, and so on. But it is also political or aes-thetico-political: Baudelaire speaks as a Frenchman surrendering to the superiority of German art, that is to say, to German music, because he is, as an exception, on a level to understand it. In this relationship also, Baudelaire again occupies a double position, as he does practically always: he is and is not French. A double posi-tion that is in reality aesthetic, and that corresponds to the oppo-sition between order and enthusiasm, between sober clarity and mystical depth. This serves to verify that the tenacious dualism of German aesthetics since Schiller, the Schlegels, or Hölderlin, which culminates or is established in the Nietzschean opposition between the Apollonian and the Dionysian, was for Baudelaire in reality the thing most immediately accessible.

This is why it is so surprising to see to what degree this letter is a pure and simple condensation of the Baudelairean aesthetic. Nothing is lacking in it: from anamnesis (I will return to this) to the sublime (the great, the high, the excessive, etc.), from "eleva-tion" to the ecstatic, from the cult of sensation to that of the imagination, from correspondences (analogy) to the bizarre, everything can be found here, or almost everything. There is even a mention of "stimulants," a Baudelairean theme if ever there was one, but a theme that Wagner invariably seems to call up, for good or bad (what is, in fact, the status of the *drug*, in Nietzsche?).

But the most definitive motif is that of *anamnesis*. If Baudelaire's subjugation is so strong, it is in reality because *he had already heard this music*: "I knew this music"; "This music was my own, and I recognized it as any man recognizes those things he is destined to love." Anamnesis is *recognition* itself; it is a matter of the *destination of the subject*.

That is the very center of the Baudelairean aesthetic, which is, as we know, an aesthetic inspired by Plato, accomplished by—at least at the beginning—a reversal of the traditional metaphysical hierarchy (between the sensible and the intelligible and, above all, good and evil), and, more importantly, also accomplished by a subjective overdetermination of ideality. This is also exactly the reason why what is demanded and sought after, in the case of anamnesis or the recourse to reminiscence, is the subject itself. Anamnesis is a case of subjective reappropriation. We should even say, more rigorously, that what is asked for is in fact the *origin* of the subject, which origin is empirically inaccessible but postulated as accessible by right (would this be the illusion of literature?), and accessible to a kind of over-memory or beyond-memory capable of gaining access to what was never present to consciousness or of returning to this side of the most primitive forgetting (the most immemorial): that is to say the forgetting of the origin itself, of who *I* was—of what "I" was—before being born, before "falling down here," being expulsed and sworn to incurable separation, to the dereliction of this world and to the interminable loss of self in triviality. This over-memory is, in other words, according to the logic of the future anterior at work in every theory of reminiscence, capable of transcending in advance death itself and finitude, the *condition* of finite being. It promises immortality.

Baudelaire, in his poems, had *already* said this.

Every time, or in any case almost every time, that the motif of anamnesis had appeared, music, perhaps under Nerval's influence (in fact it is, after Rousseau, a prominent invariable of modern *literature*), had been, if not the beginning or the motor of anamnesis, at least a major element of evocation or of the "tableau" that it brought on. As if music had always been linked to the ecstasy of reappropriation. Let us reread, specifically, "Music,"[22] despite its final fall; or even "Former Life," especially its second strophe:

> Les houles, en roulant les images des cieux,
> Mêlaient d'une façon solonnelle et mystique
> Les tout-puissants accords de leur riche musique
> Aux couleurs du couchant reflété par mes yeux.

> The swells, rolling the images of the heavens,
> Merged in a solemn and mystical way
> The all-powerful harmonies of their rich music
> With the colors of the decline reflected by my eyes.

(All its commentators have noted that this is quite close to the lexicon and the associations of the letter to Wagner.) But let us think before anything else of its metrical version in "The Invitation to the Voyage":

> Tout y parlerait
> A l'âme en secret
> Sa douce langue natale.

> Everything there would speak
> To the soul in secret
> Its sweet native tongue.

Musical reminiscence—the "I have already heard it" pronounced with amazement before Wagner's music—is this: the possibility offered to the subject to hear his native language, the language closest to his own, because the subject returned to himself is in a certain way the only reality, the absolute language. This is why the recognition—in every sense—of Wagnerian music communicates so easily with the subjective overdetermination of Baudelaire's aesthetics and poetics. With his conception of *literature*, at least in so much as this conception does not hinder the idea of poetry that Baudelaire, beyond (or on this side of) literature, humbly attempts to shape for himself.

Two proofs.

First, in the 1861 essay, when he attempts, after the program at the Théâtre des Italiens and Liszt's commentary, his own "translation" of Wagner's music, Baudelaire relates this attempt to his own theory of correspondences—borrowed, it is true, from Hoffmann—which metaphorizes, as if by chance, the phenomenon of the echo:

> The reader knows the aim we are pursuing, namely to show that true music suggests similar ideas in different minds. Moreover, *a priori* reasoning, without further analysis and without comparisons, would not be ridiculous in this context; for the only really surprising thing would be that sound *could not* suggest colour, that colours *could not* give the idea of melody, and that both sound and colour together were unsuitable as media for ideas; since all things always have been expressed by reciprocal analogies, ever since the day when God created the world as a complex indivisible totality.[23]

There follows, with no transition, the citation of the first two strophes of "Correspondences." I will cite only the second:

> Comme de long échos qui de loin se confondent
> Dans une ténébreuse et profonde unité,
> Vaste comme la nuit et comme la clarté,
> Les parfums, les couleurs et les sons se répondent.

> Like echoes which merge in the distance
> Into a unity, dark and deep,
> As measureless as night, or day,
> Scents, colours and sounds correspond.
> (trans. Charvet, p. 457n)

But above all, the translation Baudelaire proposes twice—in the letter and in the essay—coincides, in a fairly surprising way, with the famous definition of lyricism ventured in his article on Banville in *Reflections on Some of My Contemporaries.*

The letter is organized, very openly, around a thematics of the sublime. We find in it the greatness that subjugates, captivates, tears away, lifts up, ecstasy, which leads to a "broader life"; "something excessive and superlative" (the incommensurable); levitation or "elevation" that is in effect pleasure (the pleasure of comprehension but also what Nietzsche would call the hysterical pleasure of submission: "letting oneself be penetrated, invaded, a truly voluptuous sensuality"); finally, after the attempt at "visualization" (the red of passion becoming more and more ardent until the final stripes of white on white), this "supreme cry of the soul rising to its paroxysm," which is like the very moment of accession to immortality, the moment when the subject, in his deepest privacy—in his soul—is both undone and achieved: dies unto himself or fades away, to live absolutely.

It is not surprising, then, to read nearly the same thing in the essay written a few months later, an identical exercise:

> I remember the impression made upon me from the opening bars, a happy impression akin to the one that all imaginative men have known, in dreams, while asleep. I felt freed from the *constraint of weight*, and recaptured the memory of the *rare joy* that dwell in *high places* (be it noted that I had not at the time come across the programme notes I have just quoted from). Then, involuntarily, I evoked the delectable state of a man possessed by a profound reverie in total solitude, but a solitude with *vast horizons* and *bathed in a diffused light*; *immensity* without other decor than itself. Soon I became aware of a heightened *brightness*, of a *light growing in intensity* so quickly that the shades of meaning provided by a dictionary would not suffice to express this *constant increase of burning whiteness*. Then I achieved a full apprehension of a soul floating in light, of an ecstasy *compounded of joy and insight*, hovering above and far removed from the natural world. (trans. Charvet, p. 331)

This is what we will find (in sum: the accession of the soul to paradise, to the "preternatural") in the text on lyricism:

> In fact there is a lyrical manner of sensing. The men most disgraced by nature, those to whom fortune gives the least leisure, have sometimes known these sorts of impressions, so rich that the soul is as if illumi-

nated by them, so lively that it is as if lifted up by them. The whole inner being, in these marvellous instants, launches itself into the air with too much lightness and dilation, as if to attain a higher region.

Thus there also necessarily exists a lyrical manner of speaking, and a lyrical world, a lyrical atmosphere, landscapes, men, women, animals, which all participate in the personality affected by the Lyre. (2: 164)

This is a *lyrical experience*, the very experience of *transcendence*, in the active sense of the term, or, if one prefers, the *metaphysical* experience par excellence. Baudelaire, in his lexicon, speaks a little further on of *apotheosis*, which must be understood literally: "Everything . . . in the lyrical world is, so to speak, *apotheosized*." And the lyrical world is the world of the "over-human," which is reached by these "forms of language [that] naturally derive from an exaggerated excess of vitality," the forms being *hyperbole* and *apostrophe*. Thus the generality or universality of the lyrical mode— and we recognize in this without difficulty propositions very close to those that we find in Wagner: "The lyre voluntarily flees all the details that the novel delights in. The lyrical soul makes leaps as vast as syntheses. . . . It is this consideration that serves to explain to us what commodity and what beauty the poet finds in mythologies and allegories. Mythology is a dictionary of living hieroglyphs, hieroglyphs known to everyone."[24] In other words, like music for Wagner, lyricism rests upon a universal language, immediately accessible and comprehensible. Lyricism is in reality a lyric.

It is so true, Baudelaire says, that "the Lyre expresses . . . this nearly preternatural state, this intensity of life where the soul *sings*, where it is *constrained to sing*, like the tree, the bird, the sea" (2: 164). Lyricism in this sense, that is to say, *literature* according to Baudelaire, is thus nothing more than the *song of the subject*, or the subject being accomplished—by going beyond himself—as song: Baudelaire calls him "hyperbolic man," revealing himself in and through song.

This is why Baudelaire's submission to Wagner, in a first reading, the submission of "letters" to music, could only be total.

～

Such a submission, because it is thus quite profound, explains
how, at least in appearance, Baudelaire in his discourse on Wagner
at no point exceeds the limits outlined in advance by Wagner himself or by his authorized commentators, such as Liszt. In a general
way, it has often been said, the essay on Wagner is ultimately nothing but a "presentation" of Wagner, which restricts itself either to
paraphrasing for the use of the French audience, and justifying,
the great Wagnerian theories (as a sort of handy résumé of the "Letter on Music"), or to "recounting" the libretti (*Tannhäuser, Lohengrin, The Flying Dutchman*) to give the meaning of the fables.

The result: all this takes place as if Baudelaire recognized un-
conditionally the superiority of Wagnerian art and theory, or
treated Wagnerian art as this art itself in fact asks to be treated:
that is to say as achieved Art. In particular, as we have just seen
proved, everything takes place as if Baudelaire were content to say:
what I myself have attempted to do in the name of poetry or lyricism, and only by means of language, is here realized with a conjunction of means whose power is infinitely greater than that of
language alone or, worse, with a language infinitely more powerful
than language itself. That is to say, with music. From this point of
view, one could argue that it is not very difficult to show that what
Baudelaire picks up in his predilection for Wagner are above all
the themes of his own poetics. This, for example, is the reason
why he insists so much on the Wagnerian dualism (which is at
work in *Tannhäuser*: the conflict of sensuality with purity or saint-
liness, the contradiction within desire, etc.)—because he finds in it
his own motif of double "postulation."

Thus the submission is incontestable; and through it we understand that Baudelaire bequeathed to his successors, and above all
Mallarmé, this despairing idea that poetry can no longer attain
what music is capable of: or, what amounts to the same thing,
that music has, from then on, definitively relayed poetry.

Nevertheless, following the text a little more closely, we see that
things are far from being so simple and that, as a result, Baudelaire
is in reality going to bequeath a much more subtle and differenti-
ated problematic.

One of the ideas driving the essay—Baudelaire centers his conclusion around it—is in fact that Wagner can be considered "the truest representative of modern nature." Which means, more specifically, that "if by the choice of his subjects and his dramatic method, Wagner approaches antiquity," he is modern in "his expression." Yet "expression" here must be understood in two ways: it is on the one hand Wagner's privileged aesthetic mode and material, and thus it designates the music (not for an instant does Baudelaire doubt that Wagner is above all a musician); but it is also, on the other hand, the manner in which Wagner the artist expresses himself, that is to say the manifestation of his proper being, or his manifestation as the *subject* of his work (and not for an instant does Baudelaire doubt that a work of art is fundamentally the expression of a subject). Here, furthermore, is how Baudelaire begins his conclusion:

> Setting aside for the moment, as can always be done, the systematic element which every great and deliberate artist inevitably introduces into his works, we then need to seek and assess the peculiar personal qualities that distinguish him from others. An artist, a man really worthy of that great name, must surely have in him something essentially *sui generis*, by the grace of which he is himself and not someone else. . . . We have already, I think, identified two men in Richard Wagner, the man of order and the man of passion. It is the man of passion, the man of feeling, I want to discuss here. In the least of his compositions his ardent personality is so evident that this quest for his main quality will not be difficult to pursue. From the outset, one point had struck me forcefully: it is that in the sensual and orgiastic part of the *Tannhäuser* overture, the artist had put as much power, had developed as much energy, as in the description of the mysticism that characterizes the overture to *Lohengrin*; the same ambition in the one and the other, the same titanic climbing of the heights, and also the same refinements, the same subtleties. What therefore appears to me to characterize above all, and in an unforgettable way, the music of the master is nervous intensity, violence in passion and in will-power. That music expresses, now in the suavest, now in the most strident tones, all that lies most deeply hidden in the heart of man. (trans. Charvet, pp. 354–55)

The accuracy of the appreciation, though great, is of little importance here. What it says is that Wagner is essentially a *pathos*, a subject as *pathos*—which is not at all incompatible with the "will" —and that such a *pathos* defines him as "modern." This is why "all of the science, the efforts, the combinations of this rich mind"—the entire ordered, calculating, knowing, and measured side, in short the "Apollonian" side—of Wagner "are only, to tell the truth, in the humble and zealous service of this irresistible passion."

But why is this the passion that defines the modern? Because the passion, understood in Baudelaire's sense (as intensity, force, energy, or even as desire and will: these are the terms that recur most frequently), is the most hidden and therefore the most essential part "in the heart of man." In other words, passion—which is the Baudelairean word for the metaphysical concept of will, in the sense of *eros* and *appetitus*—is the essence or the identity of man determined as a subject not of representation (it is on the contrary hidden, "unconscious" as the romantics and Schopenhauer said) but of production or creation: of *poiesis*. Passion—Baudelaire says it very precisely: "passionate energy"—is the essence of the poietic subject, the only true subject in the eyes of Baudelaire. Or, what amounts to the same thing, it is the essence of "genius":

> By this passion, he adds to everything he touches an indefinable superhuman element; by this passion he understands and makes others understand everything. Everything that is implied by the words *will, desire, concentration, nervous intensity, explosion* is perceptible, may be apprehended through his works. I do not think I am deceiving myself or anybody else when I say that I see there the main characteristics of the phenomenon we call *genius*; or, at least, that in the analysis of all we have legitimately called *genius* until now, the very same characteristics are to be found. (trans. Charvet, p. 355)

This "indefinable superhuman element" that passion adds, and "genius," these are again the *topoi* of the thought of the sublime, which is decidedly the stakes of this whole confrontation. But the sublime, this time, is envisioned from the point of view of the creation, not from that of the effect produced. Via a shortcut, if you like, it is the sublime as modern poetics and then aesthetics, from Boileau to Diderot and to Kant, taking the concept—translated, reread, rewritten—from Longinus. That is to say, the sublime as it permits, on the question of "great art," the liberation from the supposedly Aristotelian dogma of *imitatio*; or rather, as it permits—by means of a subjectivist overinterpretation, it is true— the recovery of a truth of Aristotelian mimetology: that if art accomplishes or brings nature to term, it does so insofar as it proceeds with the same poietic force or with the same energy. Genius, which Longinus called a "great nature" and which Kant linked to *ingenium*, the "natural gift," is this force that in fact surpasses human resources but through which the human finds itself accomplished, in its very destination. Certainly the human is the subject. But the subject in question here, the poietic subject, exceeds the horizon of simple "subjectivity." It is a *subject in excess*, beyond the subject itself. Having taken care of the *topos*, Baudelaire knows very well what he says when he speaks of the "superhuman." The humanity of man consists in his superhumanness. Such is, in fact, the (metaphysical) lesson of the thought of the sublime.[25]

It is obviously this sort of metaphysics that explains Baudelaire's fascination with music. Only music is capable of expressing, that is to say, signifying, but beyond signification, this subjective beyond of the subject: the aspect of the subject that, in the subject and as the subject as well, moves beyond the subject.

This is not only because music defines itself as the privileged mode of the expression of feeling or even of what Baudelaire more rigorously calls "the undefined part of feeling." Although that obviously counts: for example, Baudelaire takes great care to recall, at the beginning of the second section of the essay, how Wagner himself considers that music's essential task is "to speak" feeling. And it is not without reason that he links the "Letter on Music" to Diderot:

> As I turned over the pages of the *Letter on Music*, I became aware that re-emerging in my mind, by a phenomenon of mnemonic echo, were a number of passages from Diderot, where he declares that true dra-

matic music can be nothing else than the cry or sigh of passion, translated into note and rhythmical form. (trans. Charvet, p. 335)

(Here we can see that this leads, among other things, to making music into a "dynamic" art—the lesson emphasized by romanticism—whose expressivity is linked to force or to intensity. An art of *accent*. And thus in Baudelaire's work, though less than in Wagner's, there is a relative subordination of the rhythmic element.)

But the decisive element is elsewhere: it depends on the idea that Wagner's music, more than any other, accomplishes the essence of music, that is, reveals its fundamental energetics. At no time does Baudelaire speak of "infinite melody." But we know that everything he gets from it, everything that summons him first in Wagner's music, is that this music expresses, signifies, suggests—or very directly incarnates and *presents*—the immense or the incommensurable, the excessive, the beyond of the world and of man. In short, the *infinite*. This is, he himself remarks, what makes him give a "translation" that is, as compared to those of Liszt and of Wagner himself, "much less illustrated by material objects . . . , more vague and more abstract" (2: 785). By this, Baudelaire not only means to signify that he remains relatively indifferent to *Lohengrin*'s Saint-Sulpicien grab bag, which is otherwise apparent. By this he also wants to show, in retaining only the "resemblances" of the three translations—"numerous and captivating even to the point of superfluity"—that the music of Wagner has the effect of suggesting a certain type of *sensation*.

> In the three translations we find the sensation of *spiritual and physical beatitude*; of *isolation*; of the contemplation of *something infinitely great and infinitely beautiful*; in an *intense light* that pleases *the eyes and the soul to the point of swooning*; and finally the sensation of *space stretched to the ultimate conceivable limits*.
>
> No musician excels, as Wagner does, at *painting* material and spiritual space and depth.

Inasmuch as he speaks in terms of sensation and sensual qualities, Baudelaire, who in this way might once more justify the universal character of musical language, makes music into the *aesthetic* language par excellence and, in the same stroke, the art in which the *aesthetic function*, in general, is accomplished. This is why music, with this authority, completes and brings together art in its aesthetic definition, to which Baudelaire submits most of the time. In any case sensation, for Baudelaire, is divided: strangely, it is simultaneously spiritual and physical, or material. So that it is very difficult to understand to what *sensual content*, as *sensation*, it in fact gives access. This will work for light, since it delights the soul as much as the eyes. But beatitude and isolation? The "something infinitely great and infinitely beautiful." In reality music suggests no sensual quality, even one that is "pure," like light (or even like the incandescence that the letter spoke of). Or if it does so, it is only very secondarily, that is to say, inasmuch as one is content with the *aesthetic* of correspondences, which is perhaps not, at any rate not from this point of view, the essential one in Baudelaire. Neither does music simply evoke the suprasensual or the metaphysical as such, despite the fact that, as Kant would have said, it brings it into thought. What it offers, first of all, without properly presenting it, is the pure form *a priori* of sensual intuition—space, here depth—which is in effect neither material nor spiritual.

Music, in other words, carries *aisthesis* to its limit: it gives the sensation, infinitely paradoxical, of the condition of all sensation, as if the impossible task of presenting the transcendental, that is to say the pure possibility of presentation itself, in general, were incumbent upon it. Moreover, that is very much why, at this limit, music does not cease to indicate the unlimited (the infinite) that contains it at its outer edge. This is in fact its sublime vocation.[26] And it is equally why, even if Baudelaire is a victim of the (aesthetic) *religion* of Wagner (even if he exhausts himself in particular with justifying the recourse to myth),[27] he only retains, ultimately, what in Wagner's music exceeds the *musica ficta*. Representation, in the sense that one can call it the *stile rappresentativo*, culminates in Wagner; but also, in the sense that this music needs a theater, images, and illustration, it does not actually interest Baudelaire. And thus in the end, his Wagner is not Wagner.

~

Suspicion begins to take shape if we notice that Baudelaire, almost systematically, continuously draws out from the motifs of the infinite, of immensity, of grandeur or the excess of grandeur, an idea of the *ecstatic*, in the strictest sense. "Sensation" is ecstasy. I mean: there where Wagner's indications or Liszt's commentary should suggest that he translate in terms of felicity and beatitude, accomplishment, plenitude, the return to self or reappropriation of the soul exalted by music, Baudelaire regularly translates in terms of failure (or fainting), excessive and unbearable *jouissance*, and being beside oneself. Or of pure joy, which is completely disruptive or destructive. Such things are certainly not unknown in Wagner. But for Baudelaire it is as if the effect of music were necessarily abyssal—"vertiginous," he says, when he compares it to the effects of opium.[28] Listening is an ordeal of dispossession or deappropriation. Not a matter of pleasure, but of *jouissance*, in the sense of Barthes's use of Lacan's word. It is detachment from self, the exposition of the original horror and pain, already quite close to what Nietzsche will try to theorize as Dionysiac ecstasy or tragic vertigo. For Baudelaire, such is Tannhäuser—and his listener—who, "saturated with enervating pleasures, aspires to suffering!" "A sublime cry," adds Baudelaire, who knows perfectly what he is talking about, that is, who knows perfectly, and not only because he comes after Burke, to what degree pain is consubstantial with the sublime.

But this *jouissance* is in turn linked to the body, or rather, to flesh, as Baudelaire says without departing from his impeccable precision. Again, on *Tannhäuser*, he writes:

> In the *Tannhäuser* overture, in the struggle between the two opposing principles, he [Wagner] has shown himself no less subtle or powerful. Whence, one may ask, has the master drawn this frenzied song of the flesh, this total knowledge of the diabolical element in man? From the very first bars our nerves vibrate in unison with the melody; any flesh that remembers itself begins to tremble. . . . First come the satanic titillations of a vague love, soon followed by enticements, swoonings, cries of victory, groans of gratitude, then again ferocious howls, victims' curses, impious hosannas from those officiating at the

sacrifice, as though barbarism must always have its place in the drama of love, and the enjoyment of the flesh must lead, by an inescapable satanic logic, to the delights of crime.[29]

Of course, Baudelaire does not permit himself in any way to let the fable of *Tannhäuser* pass without commentary: he cannot make the libretto or the music say what they do not say. So he underlines the presence of the second theme, religious and appeasing; he recognizes the motif of the return to self—and to the native or the "naive": "poor humanity . . . returned to its fatherland." Manifestly, however, it is the demoniac, satanic, carnal theme that keeps his whole attention—and, most of all, his writer's attention. Baudelaire is not content with recognizing, which is already a lot, that probably no music more than Wagner's knows how to translate carnal feeling or erotic ecstasy (and again we should not forget that he was only familiar with the prelude of *Tristan*). But what he is trying to *write* for his record is the "chaos of agonistic sensualities," it is this *emotion* itself, in its literal sense, or this ecstasy. On the other hand, when he arrives at the second theme, the "beatitude of redemption," he limits himself to speaking from some distance (and in a fairly conventional manner) of "ineffable feeling," and he returns, in the style of simple description, to the libretto's indications: he tells a story.

In other words, Baudelaire *writes* Wagner. In any case, this is not at all surprising if, in its most "inspired" moments, this critical prose equals that of the "Prose Poems," which are probably, in Baudelaire, what exceeds or are on the way to exceeding *literature*, that is, the lyrical in its subjective determination. Another lyricism begins to be invented with Baudelaire. In particular, but not only, in the "translation" into prose of certain poems from *The Flowers of Evil*—even though, certainly, *everything* here is a matter of *translation*—in a new sense, as attested by the task of the translator that Baudelaire assigns himself and the very high idea he holds of critical writing. This other lyricism, which cannot properly be called objective, does not at all reverse the values of lyricism but leaves perfectly intact their entire thematics. It is simply the *rewriting*— the translation—of lyricism itself, whose *aura* he withholds for this reason. One might say that he desacralizes lyricism. It would be more correct to say that he *literalizes* it: he destroys it, through cold, deliberate, calculated explication and recomposition; figural deportation or "transportation." He corrodes metaphor at the very time when he must, under the sign of the loss of the "grand art," admit to the impossible presentation of the metaphysical and when he submits to all the rigor of the sublime. Benjamin, who described this movement better than anyone, wrestled away from speculative romanticism—thanks, it is true, to Hölderlin, specifically to his translations of Sophocles—this intuition that "the Idea of poetry is prose." And he retained Hölderlin's word *sobriety*, which, in his eyes, defined not only the modern (in its opposition to ancient "enthusiasm" or, as Baudelaire called it, "apotheosis") but the entire, as yet uncertain, future of literature, or of what we have learned to call, with difficulty, and never in a definitive nor decisive way, *écriture*.[30]

Such a step was taken, imperceptibly, when the *lyric* of Wagner restrained the lyricism of Baudelaire.

The reason for it could be this: musical signification—that which, in music, goes beyond signification (the "fiction") and, to this extent, for those who wish to translate it, can only be brought out by *écriture*, not by effusion or a review—this signification refers less to the soul in excess than to the body in excess, that is to say to the flesh, which, however, in no way lacks soul. A certain materiality of the spiritual itself is involved here. Whence Baudelaire's insistence on spatiality, depth, immensity: listening engenders a co-anaesthetic phenomenon, not because the body (or the soul) is equal to the All into which it melts (as Isolde sings at the end of Tristan) but because the psyche, as Freud says in an enigmatic note, reveals itself as "spread out." In this moment the sensual moves outside the self, *physis* is transcended—and Baudelaire is right to speak of the "preternatural." But this preternatural does not create any other world. The metaphysical, understood with all rigor, is here below, at the heart of things and of the flesh. From this insight comes the idea that lyrical prose, more systematically than poems, must accomplish the alliance of two lexicons, the moral and the natural (or the ideal and the real), as Baudelaire ultimately gives an example of when he describes the erotic agon that suggests the "black" theme of *Tannhäuser* ("groans of gratitude," "victims' curses," "impious hosannas from those officiating at the sacrifice," etc.). From this insight comes as well the idea that musical signification, as a note of "My Heart Laid Bare" reminds us, stems, finally, less from an energetics (accent or intensity) than from a fundamental prosody or rhythmics:

> Music gives the idea of space.
> All the arts, more or less; because they are *number* and number is a translation of space. (2: 702)

But first of all another consequence will be brought to light. It will touch on the constitution of the lyric subject.

It is not much to say that, under his apparent submission, Baudelaire continuously works on a veritable "Baudelairianization" of Wagner, if we can authorize this term. I will give only one example. It takes us back again to the evocation of the demoniac theme of *Tannhäuser*, when Baudelaire awakens, in such a striking manner, a memory of the flesh:

> From the very first bars our nerves vibrate in unison with the melody; any flesh that remembers itself begins to tremble. Every well-ordered brain has within it two infinities, heaven and hell; and in any image of one of these it suddenly recognizes the half of itself.[31]

The Baudelairean metaphysics of "double postulation" upholds the music of Wagner. And thus the act. In fact, Baudelaire has always already told the truth of Wagner. Retrospectively, moreover, this "coincidence" permits the clarification of what Baudelaire uncovers as the apportionment of the classical and the romantic, or the modern, in Wagner. I am thinking in particular of the very detailed passage that Baudelaire devotes, in the second section, to the "dramatic ideal" of Wagner, to his deliberate borrowings from the Greek construction of tragedy, and where he sketches, in his manner, a history of aesthetic dualism, that is to say of what will become the duality or antagonism of the Apollonian and the Dionysian. In his manner, that is, through the intervention of Christianity—and consequently of evil. Baudelaire drags Wagner onto the side of his "Catholic" aesthetic:

> The radiant Venus of antiquity, Aphrodite, born of the white sea-foam, has not crossed the horrific shades of the Middle Ages with impunity. No longer does she inhabit Olympus or the shores of some sweet-smelling archipelago. She has withdrawn into a cavern, admittedly magnificent, but illuminated by fires other than those of the kindly Phoebus. In going underground Venus has come nearer to hell, and, no doubt, on the occasion of certain abominable solemnities she goes and pays regular homage to the Arch-demon, prince of the flesh and lord of sin. Similarly Wagner's poems, although they show a genuine liking for classical beauty and a perfect understanding of it, also have a strong admixture of the romantic spirit. They may suggest to us the majesty of Sophocles and Aeschylus, but they also forcefully recall to our minds the mystery plays of the period when Catholicism was dominant in the plastic arts. They are like those great visions that the Middle Ages spread out on the walls of its churches or wove into its magnificent tapestries. They have a decidedly legendary aspect. (trans. Charvet, pp. 337–38)

This insistence on the Christian thematics in no way betrays Wagner himself, and scarcely accentuates the antecedence, already underlined by Wagner, of legend to myth and the substitution of the Christian scenario for the properly tragic scenario. But it permits Baudelaire to introduce, beyond the most explicit intentions of Wagner, the idea of a divided subject, torn (ripped apart) or even, more precisely, quartered, and thus with no possibility of self-reconciliation. The Baudelairean subject, unlike the Wagnerian, only finds "half of himself" in the image he carries within himself of two infinities, heaven and hell. Unity is impossible for him: it is either heaven or hell, but never the one *as* the other nor, even less, one as the sublation of the other. And moreover, it is rather always hell, in spite of the vague inclination for sainthood and the promises of efforts to be made. If Baudelaire is sensitive to the "voluptuous part" of the overture of *Tannhäuser* to this degree, to the detriment of the libretto's lesson, this in fact credits Wagner, in a very surprising fashion, with a sort of "negative" mysticism, which is that of *Flowers of Evil* or of the "Personal Diaries." Manifestly, what Baudelaire *recognizes* in Wagner is not there: because it is not redemption but the intuition of an absolute that is attained, *reached* within evil. That is to say also within the most serious, the most desperate loss of self—whether by error or by fault matters little. Weakness, at any rate, even if it gives way to heroism itself:

> Just now, as I was trying to describe the sensual part of the overture, I asked the reader to close his mind to commonplace love songs such as a swain in high spirits might conceive them; and certainly there is nothing trivial here; rather is it the overflowing of a powerful nature, pouring into evil all the strength it should devote to the cultivation of good; it is love, unbridled, vast, chaotic, raised to the height of an anti-religion, a satanic religion. Thus in his musical interpretation the composer has avoided the vulgarity that too often accompanies the expression of the feeling, of all feelings—the most popular—I nearly said "of the populace"—and to achieve that all he had to do was to express the overabundance of desire and energy, the indomitable, unrestrained ambition of a delicate soul that has taken the wrong road. (trans. Charvet, pp. 343–44)

Under the appearance of the most faithful reading of and the most scrupulous attention to Wagner's text, critical or poetic, there is in reality here a real *perversion* of Wagner. Which takes place, exclusively, through the interpretation of Wagner's *music*: what this music signifies is essentially what Baudelaire's writing wants to signify, that which, beyond lyricism in its simple modern definition, transcribes—or provokes—the "dissociation" of the subject.[32]

Thus when Baudelaire subscribes to the Wagnerian theorem according to which music "complements" poetry, we have to look more closely. What in fact does Baudelaire say?

> [W]ithout the poetry Wagner's music would still be a poetic work, endowed as it is with all the qualities that go to make a well-organized poem; self-explanatory, so well are its component parts united, integrated, mutually adapted, and, if I may invent a word to express the superlative of a quality, prudently *concatenated*. (trans. Charvet, p. 351)

We imagine that this is a very familiar idea: if Wagner's music, by
itself, is poetic, this is because it is, in itself, systematic. Its basic
"organicity" allowed him to effectuate the Work of Art, in absolute
terms, and to complete art in its essence, that is to say as *poiesis*. Yet
this is not at all what Baudelaire says. In fact, this remark inter-
cedes as a commentary on the citation of a long page of Liszt
where he explains how Wagner's music can awaken signification
(this time in the intellectual sense), namely, by substituting for the
function of discourse and language, and articulating itself as a veritable syntax. It is evidently a question of the technique of the leitmotiv. Liszt describes it thus:

> By means of a technique which he applies in a wholly unexpected
> way, Wagner succeeds in extending the sway and the claims of music.
> Not content merely with the power it exercises on the heart of man by
> awakening the whole scale of human sentiments, he enables it to stim-
> ulate our ideas, to speak to our minds, to appeal to our power of re-
> flexion, he endows it with a moral and intellectual significance. He
> outlines melodically the character of his heroes and heroines and their
> main passions, and these melodic themes emerge, *in the vocal part or
> in the accompaniment*, every time the passions and feelings they ex-
> press come into play.[33]

Baudelaire, then, very accurately speaks of music, of the musical
"system" of Wagner, in terms of "concatenation." And very accurately, too, he links the procedure both to the Wagnerian recourse
to myth (myth is itself the product of "motifs" that Baudelaire understands as allegorical and symbolic) and to the style of scenic
presentation, that is to say to the scenic incarnation of mythemes
in characters, actions, or situations. Thus he can write that "each
character is, so to speak, emblazoned by the melody that represents his moral character and the part he is called on to play in the
fable" (trans. Charvet, p. 348).

    Music is thus only language, it only signifies inasmuch as it has
the power to "emblazon" or emblematize. I would rather say: to
type, in the sense where this word, in Greek, designates the imprint, the mark impressed by a seal, the striking. German translates
it as "prägen" ("Prägung") and we know that this term, in the tra-

dition of speculative idealism, serves to designate the mode of appearance and production of the figure, the Gestalt.[34] In this sense, and if we are guided in French by the derivations of the Latin *fingere*, Wagner's music is a figural music (Nietzsche will speak of Hegelian contamination), and in it, in fact, *musica ficta* is accomplished. It is certainly also why it is indissociable from a *fiction* and is definitively sustained by a mythology. But this is not exactly what Baudelaire means, although he knows, yet again, that it is in fact so and that he even guesses to what point the Wagnerian system is of a "structural" order, as Lévi-Strauss will later demonstrate. A different suspicion emerges in his commentary. As if Baudelaire knew obscurely that, just as heraldry implies writing and just as there is a semantics and a syntax of blazons, type is also character—or *letter*. If we consider that the letter in archaic Greek (that of Democritus, for example) could also be called *rhythmos*, we begin to dream: might Baudelaire have tried to imagine, beyond Wagner's most manifest intentions, something like the *rhythmic* essence of music? Might the recurrent melody, in Wagner's "mnemonic" system, have functioned as the letter, and might music, in signifying, have been a sort of writing? On this account, Baudelaire's silence on the "infinite melody" could in effect be the index of a will to the literalization of the music.

Baudelaire would certainly never have expressed himself in these terms, which will be Mallarmé's. It is clear that, in any case, on the question of music, he never went beyond the relatively conventional consideration of number. Yet he will have *recognized* in Wagner's music, explicitly, a quality that made it to his eyes the *equal* of poetry: that of being able to *present ideas*, something like the way in which Liszt said that certain melodic sections, in Wagner, are the "personifications of ideas." From there, finally, he conceded that music, in its modern development, had known how to raise itself to the height of the "philosophical" vocation, that is, the vocation of the *savant*, which for him was that of true poetry, from the beginning. But that was only the case inasmuch as the melody-ideas of this sort of music-writing were "prudently concatenated." In other words, the sign was quite clear all the same; it was less the

§2 Mallarmé

Car il faut la mort pour savoir le Mystère.
Because death is necessary to understand the Mystery.

—Mallarmé

Le silence déjà funèbre d'une moire
Dispose plus qu'un pli seul sur le mobilier
Que doit un tassement du principal pilier
Précipiter avec le manque de mémoire.

Notre si vieil ébat triomphal du grimoire
Hiéroglyphes dont s'exalte le millier
A propager de l'aile un frisson familier!
Enfouissez-le-moi plutôt dans un armoire.

Du souriant fracas originel haï
Entre elles de clartés maîtresses a jailli
Jusque vers un parvis né pour leur simulacre,

Trompettes tout haut d'or pâmé sur les vélins,
Le dieu Richard Wagner irradiant un sacre
Mal tu par l'encre même en sanglots sibyllins.

The already funereal silence of moiré
Disposes [of] more than a single fold over the space
Than a piling up of the principal pillar must
Precipitate with the lack of memory.

Our very old triumphal conquest of the magic book,
Hieroglyphs in which the many exalt
In propagating with the wing a familiar frisson!
I'd rather you buried them in an armoire.

From the smiling, hated, originary fracas,
Amongst themselves, masterful clarities
To a parvis created for their simulacrum,

Golden trumpets on high fading on vellum,
Surged the god Richard Wagner irradiating a ritual
Badly silenced by ink even in sibylline sobbing.

—Mallarmé

Mallarmé knows that the very serious conflict that pits him against Wagner is in some part, perhaps the essential part, a legacy. His aggravation of it, moreover, is the necessary condition for fidelity. Not to a particular man, as yet unknown, or even to a particular oeuvre—even if it sketched the promise of the "Volume." But to the very project of Poetry, or of what he called, in a sense that was his, Literature. And to a language, that is—the word recurs often—to a "race," which we should translate as "people" or "nation." Because in the case of Wagner, it was in fact a *challenge* that Baudelaire took on; and Mallarmé felt it necessary to draw out its consequences.

Several of his paragraphs signal this with the most straightforward precision:

> Even in the work of Wagner, for the incomplete invocation of which here the most superbly French poet makes up, I do not perceive the theater in its strict acceptation (without contest we will find more, from the point of view of drama, in Greece or in Shakespeare), but legendary vision, self-sufficient under the veil of sonorities and merging into it; moreover, neither are its partitions, compared to Beethoven or Bach, simply music. Something special and complex results: located at the convergences of the other arts, coming out of them and governing them: Fiction or Poetry.[1]

> A singular challenge that Richard Wagner inflicts on poets, whose duty he usurps with the most candid and splendid bravura!
>
> Feelings about this foreigner become complicated—transports, veneration, as well as a malaise that everything be done, not by radiating out, but by a direct play of the literary principle itself.[2]

Mallarmé's question—because there is a question, obstinately posed—is here in its entirety: to whom does it fall to accomplish, and to represent, art? Who, definitively, is in charge of *poesis*, or *mousikè*, which is more or less its equivalent: the musician or the poet?

The scene is very old, and nearly inaugural: Mallarmé is barely twenty years old, has not heard a note of Wagner (but it is 1862 and he has just read, one after the other, the reedition of Baudelaire's *The Flowers of Evil* and his important 1861 essay on Wagner), and it is just at this time that he begins to publish; he sends to *L'Artiste* a text, a fairly violent polemic, that he calls "Artistic Heresies—Art for All."

It begins:

> Everything sacred and wishing to remain sacred is enveloped in mystery. Religions take refuge in the shelter of secrets unveiled only to the predestined: art has its own.
>
> Music gives us an example. Opening Mozart, Beethoven, or Wagner at will, looking over the first page of their work with an indifferent eye, we are overtaken by a religious astonishment at the sight of these macabre processions and severe, chaste, unknown signs. And we close up the missal, virgin of any profaning thought.
>
> I have often asked why this necessary trait has been refused to a single art, the greatest. This one is without mystery to counter hypocritical curiosity, or terror to counter the impious, or under the smile and the grimace of the ignorant and the enemy.
>
> I am speaking of poetry.[3]

And as an example of the profaned poetic "mystery," Mallarmé immediately cites, of course, *The Flowers of Evil*: nothing distinguishes it materially (that is to say spiritually, as well) from any ordinary publication, consequently nothing protects it against any ordinary intrusions: "Thus the first-comers enter a masterpiece on the same footing." This is the legacy of Baudelaire, but it is as if Mallarmé were unaware of it: poetry must have this "caractère nécessaire," this "necessary trait," the lack of which causes it to remain unrecognized as the greatest of all arts. And the text is known, moreover, for its surprising programmatic precision, even in its lexicon. A few lines further, Mallarmé laments that an "immaculate language" has never been invented since poetry has existed ("the arid study of hieratic formulae that blinds the profane and needles the fatal patient"); he dreams of books consecrated by an interdiction: "O golden clasps on old missals! O unravished hieroglyphs of papyrus rolls!" On this subject Mallarmé will never change: this will remain his intransigent Idea of Art. Which is to say, Poetry.

What is surprising here is that the first intuition of what will end up being called, in fact, Mystery, comes exclusively from the confrontation between music and poetry; and that the name of Wagner is thus connected with it from the beginning. Because if there is a program, it is not simply one for the "Volume," and even less—it goes without saying—for a supposed "hermetism." It is rather for an *agôn* that will continue to the end, without respite. Everything happens as if the project of Mallarmé has its origin in Baudelaire's recognition of Wagner.

Proof? In the lecture on Villiers de l'Isle-Adam of 1890:

> It seems that by some order of the literary mind, and by forethought, at the precise moment when music seems to suit, better than any rite, what is contained, latent and forever abstruse, in the presence of a crowd, it has been shown that nothing exists, in the inarticulation or anonymity of these cries, jubilation, swells, and all transports, that can with magnificence equal or better our conscience, this clarity, render the old and sainted elocution; or the Word, when it is someone who offers it.[4]

Variations on a Subject, 1895:

> Writing, rarefied not long ago by the symphony . . .
>
> I know, they want to limit the mystery of Music, when writing lays claim to it.
>
> Poetry, close to *idea*, is Music, par excellence—concedes no inferiority.[5]

And again, a little earlier, where the agon was clearly designated, and accepted—"Floorboards and folios," in *Sketched at the Theater*:

> Everything, the magnificent instrumental polyphony, the living gesture or the voices of characters and gods, moreover an excess brought to the material decoration, in the triumph of genius, with Wagner, we consider, dazzled by such cohesion, or art, that today becomes poetry: will it be that the traditional writer of verse, he who holds himself to the humble and sacred artifice of words, will try, according to his unique, subtly chosen resource, to rival this! Yes. (p. 328)

In this way the citations could be multiplied. Nothing was repeated more obstinately by Mallarmé; as if, between "Richard Wagner: Reverie of a French Poet" and *Music and Letters*, everything, or almost everything, was collected and comprehended in a project that seems to have found its origin in the "singular challenge" launched by Wagner. The conflict is thus in fact very serious. Which does not mean, for all that, that the dispute is simple.

⁓

Wagner, he had said in substance in "Solemnity," is neither really theater nor properly music. And reference was made to the Greeks and Shakespeare, or to Bach and Beethoven. There was nothing critical in this; on the contrary, he described there, in his way, what Wagner himself envisioned under the name of *Gesamt-kunstwerk*, even if Mallarmé did not place it under the authority of music: "Something special and complex results: situated at the convergences of the other arts, issuing from them and governing them, Fiction or Poetry" (p. 335). In the same way, "Floorboards and Folios" spoke of "a . . . cohesion, or an art, which today becomes poetry" (p. 328). And if it is important to hear in "fiction" the Latin *fingere*, it is also useful to let resonate in "art," translated by "cohesion"—or translating it—the first meaning of *ars*: articulation or juncture, adjustment, fitting together—what in Greek, ultimately, one would have called "system." But on what condition, according to his announcement, can poetry thus understood occur? On what condition is it possible that "Music has joined verse to form, since Wagner, Poetry"?[6] First, on the condition, precisely, that a "cohesion" is established between music and theater. The "Reverie" on Wagner sketched the problem in these terms:

> Omission made of glances at the extraordinary but today unfinished splendor of plastic figuration, from which, at least, in its perfected rendering, is isolated the Dance, which is alone capable, in its summary writing, of translating the fleeting and the sudden up to the Idea—same vision comprehends all, absolutely all the future Spectacle—this amateur, if he envisions the contribution of Music to Theater, made to mobilize its marvel, does not long dream apart from self . . . already, with what bounds his thought departs, feeling the

colossal approach of an Initiation. Your wish, rather, see if it is not rendered.

Singular challenge, etc. (p. 541)

That Mallarmé declares "plastic figuration" unfinished, even in its profusion, accords fairly well, all things considered, with what Baudelaire might have been thinking several years earlier, when he bluntly declared to Manet that he was after all only "the first in the decrepitude of [his] art." Modern art—as it was being born—left perplexed even those who were among the most aware or the most attentive. On the other hand, that Mallarmé thus detaches the dance, or "isolates" it—this gesture, also frequent, belongs only to him. We see in passing that this art is essentially *écriture*, and that it is also its vocation to "translate the fleeting and the sudden up to the Idea." Whence we will concede without difficulty to Alain Badiou that there is clearly a Mallarméan poetics of the event.[7] Having said this, let us not too quickly ironize the "prophetic tone" in which it is announced that the "same vision," after the dance, "comprehends all, absolutely all the future Spectacle." The transports toward the Idea, conforming to the origin of the word, imply that vision—spectacle—is not unessential to art—on the contrary. In reality, from this it follows that the theater and more generally every *theoretical* mode of presentation are constitutive of what must be called the ideal of art. "The theater is, in its essence, superior" says a text of *Sketched at the Theater*.[8] However, beyond what the ballet allows only a presentiment of, the theater, inasmuch as the musical "addition" "mobilizes its marvel," is Wagner's site. And the occasion for an "Initiation"—the word is not lightly used. "Nearly a Ritual!" says Mallarmé when he invokes, at the beginning of the "Reverie," what the "sovereign pomp of Poetry" should be. It is a matter of the sacred itself. Religion—and art, Mallarmé does not doubt for one instant, is religion—requires, obviously under some conditions, a theater. As if religion were in essence theatrical, or, inversely, theater in essence religious.

In what sense, consequently, must we understand "theater" here?

Behind the very lofty idea of theater that Mallarmé makes for himself, there is first, for the whole epoch as well as for Wagner

himself, Mallarmé knows perfectly well, the Greek example: tragedy. Just after indicating what Mystery must consist in—briefly, as
against the *Festspiel*—Mallarmé, again in the "Reverie," refers to
tragedy: it is the origin, precisely the one that Wagner does not
overtake if, in his work, "everything soaks in the primitive stream:
not back at its source."

> The City, which gave for the sacred experience a theater, imprints on
> the earth the universal seal.
>
> As to its people, it is really the least that it witnessed the august
> fact, I attest to the Justice that can only reign there! because this or-
> chestration, from which, a moment ago, came the evidence of god,
> never synthesizes anything other than the immortal, innate delicacy
> and magnificence that are unknown to all in the concourse of a mute
> audience. (p. 545)

This is very precisely the "religion of art," in the sense in which the
Phenomenology of Spirit sets forth the concept. But such a religion
of art does not in any way make a "moment," even though it virtually contains catholicity as such, and thus differs from what happens in Hegel. It is clear, de facto, that the inaugural link between
theater and "sacred experience," forged by the Greeks, has remained unbroken. The mark of Athens is definitive; we might call
it "historial":[9] it has once and for all sealed the destiny of religion
and produced the form of all ceremonial, that is to say of all presentation, if there is a *presentation*, of the divine. Assuredly—it is
equally clear—the stage itself does not suffice for this; neither consequently does the theater if it ends up being reduced to a stage.
The god arises from music (and dance), from the place of the
orkhestra; and because it is a question of origin, Mallarmé knows
well that tragedy has to be led back to the chorus and its all-pow-
erful lyricism. That is why, as to *representation* itself, and the type
of participation that it commands, he always shows some reticence.
Thus, for example, in "Catholicism" (where it is a question, once
again, of identifying the Mystery):

> Mystery, other than representational and, I would say, Greek, Play,
> mass. You sense as more "objective," detached, illusory, at the ancient

games, Prometheus himself, Orestes, it was the custom to envelop the
steps with legends, whose frisson remained, certainly, in the spectators' dresses but, without terror in this fold, that such a grandiloquent
vicissitude affected whoever contemplated it, as a protagonist unbeknownst to himself.[10]

There is thus a rigid distinction between the *skena* and the *orkhestra*, and it is also on this—to which I will return—that the distinction between legend and myth is built, a distinction that Baudelaire did not really make. For this reason, Mallarmé detaches the
"orchestration" from the tragic mode inasmuch as it offers the
purest form of the rite, as the mass that derives from it proves.

The essential thing in ceremony (in celebration) is the *unknown*:
the word Mystery is not pronounced in vain.

The legacy of Athens: the theater—the sacred experience—is
the assembly, on certain special occasions (in festival time, as compared to ordinary existence), of a crowd; that is to say, in ideal
terms, of a people, around the enigma that as a crowd it creates,
and around the secret, always already revealed, of the transcendence that constitutes it, in the profoundest depths of its imma-
nence, and whose meaning the crowd secretly holds. The essential
thing in theater is thus what Mallarmé's lecture on Villiers calls
"the latent and forever abstruse contained in the presence of the
crowd," or the "Reverie," more summarily, "the meaning latent in
the concurrence of everyone." (But this motif, as we know, is omnipresent.) Such a meaning, immemorially buried in the human
heart (immortal, innate), lies simply in what obliges us to assem-
ble. In *religare* itself. It is "unconscious" or "unknown." It does not
get revealed, it is present—without presenting itself—and it is
marked by this: the meditation of the group, a "solemnity," a frisson and something like a voiceless terror. Unease [*émoi*] more than
emotion. And the sacred, I might say, resides in this secret. Such is
the reason why, as Mallarmé says in "The Same" (and that in this
context it is about Catholicism makes no difference), "it was impossible that into religion . . . the race did not put its private, unknown secret."[11] Religion is, first of all, nothing other than the
preservation—and the celebration—of the unknown.

Thus no faith or belief, no adhesion, is in play here (the constraint of the unknown is absolutely anterior). But rather a vertigo, facing the being-there-together. That is why the unknown is this from the very beginning, that is to say from the fact that *there exist* human beings and what binds them to the core of one community or another according to one language or another. As "Sacred Pleasure" says, the "function par excellence" of the crowd is to be "the keeper of its mystery! Its own!"[12] But this is so also as a consequence of a god, if ultimately this god is nothing but the astonishment of humans before precisely this: that there are human beings and language—nations and tongues. The incomprehensible itself. A sentence of "Catholicism"—about which I will reserve commentary for the moment, says this:

> In some amphitheater, like a wing of human infinity, the multitude bifurcates, startled before the brusque abyss made by god, man—or Type. (p. 393)

This abyss is mystery itself and for Mallarmé it defines "grandeur," if mystery is "what is in the world in order to envisage grandeur" ("Genre or On Moderns," p. 314). It is the meta-physical as such— Mallarmé comes to use the word—or, in the most literal sense, "magnificence." And in consequence, not surprisingly, it is "sublimity."

This means that the theater, in Mallarmé's sense, has in no way as its vocation to engage an adhesion by one mode or another of participation or identification. It is not an Aristotelian theater: neither *mimesis* nor, consequently, *katharsis* is essential to it. In "Catholicism," when Mallarmé, in order to evoke tragedy, condenses the *Poetics* into four lines, we see clearly that the complaint about representational distance and, at the same time, about the stage illusion and the drama itself (about "legends") is in reality a complaint about a purgation or purification by means of a purely homeopathic dose: the "frisson in the spectator's dresses" is "without terror in this fold," and the spectator is not the "protagonist unbeknownst to himself." The theater of Mallarmé is sustained by a completely different—and otherwise exclusive—claim to the ab-

solute. From which comes, also, the unpitiable critique of semblance and of all forms of projection and empathy (I will not say
"communion"). Mallarmé is opposed, in principle and with rigor,
to everything that could come from a "hysterical" conception of
theater. He does not have, in this regard in any case, the least Wagnerian weakness. Certainly, his theater convokes a crowd. This is
not the same, even at the embryonic state, as a mass spectacle—
which is, finally, what Wagner aims for. It is true that there is an
eminently political destination for theater. As with Wagner, it is,
always, a matter of religion. But "political" is here to be taken in a
strict sense. The great art that Mallarmé imagines is an art of the
State, a *civic* art, with no temptation to demagoguery. We get a
clear idea of it when he protests with the last energy, that is to say
with a certain violence, precisely against the deteriorating modern
State's lack of grandeur, and its distressing "laicity," in the name of
the properly religious conception that he makes for himself of the
City. The theater of the bourgeois era manifestly missed its mark:
it is nothing but a very vague site of pleasure. There is sufficient
reason to demand of the State that it restore to theater its primary
vocation. Without doubt an analogous movement is sketched in
Wagner. But Wagner thinks, above all, in terms of people, even—
in a way that is not very Mallarméan—of race; and it is not to the
State as such that he addresses himself. Without counting the fact
that he had lost, after 1848, the social memory that Mallarmé had
kept since 1870 and that makes him speak, with the greatest precision, of the "social diminution," of "unexplained sacrifices" or of
"insignificance," and of the "mediocre exterior at present sustained
and accepted by the individual" ("Sacred Pleasure," p. 390). I cite
without commentary, as it is so clear:

> The stage is the obvious foyer of pleasures taken in common; also
> and very well thought out, the majestic opening onto the mystery
> whose grandeur one is in the world to envisage, the very mystery that
> the citizen who has an idea of it founds the right to claim from a
> State, as compensation for social diminution. So one figures the gov-
> erning entity otherwise than as annoyed (the royal puppets of the
> past, they unknowingly guaranteed what was laughable in their berib-

boned personage with their silent humbug; but now simple generals)
by a pretension of the ill-bred to pomp, to resplendency, to some solemnization of the God that he knows to be! ("Genre or On Moderns," p. 314)

Or again:

> The State, by reason of unexplained sacrifices required of the indi-
> vidual and consequently arising from faith, or our insignificance, owes
> pageantry: unlikely in fact, in that we are, vis-à-vis the absolute, the
> misters that we ordinarily appear. Some royalty environed by mili-
> tary prestige, formerly publicly sufficient, has ceased: and the ortho-
> doxy of our secret élans, which perpetuates itself, returned to the
> clergy, suffers from etiolation. ("The Same," p. 395)

Tragedy, however, is not the entire ceremonial. It is necessary to
measure the emergence of the modern—and there again the prox-
imity with Wagner is patent. However, as is said in "Magic," "The
middle age, incubatory: everything since, alloy with the antique, to
compose this vain, perplex, escaping us, modernity—further the
petrified Roman legislation stagnates a religion, that of the cathe-
drals, in parallel."[13] Or in "Catholicism," more abruptly: "The
middle age, for ever, remains the incubation as well as the commencement of the modern world" (p. 392). For ever, that is to say
that irreversibly, from now on, another religion—even if it be used
up—is ours, a different ritual substituted for the previous one. The
"catholicity" of Athens does not in any way prevent this modifica-
tion, which is itself also historial. As Wagner will end up being
convinced—but the model was programmatically patented in the
last lines of Schelling's *Philosophy of Art* in 1802—the mass has in
reality *become* the prototype of the absolute work of art.

But it is still, of course, theater.

This is what "Catholicism" and "The Same" explain, in a detailed way. Possibly nowhere else—even considering the already
impressive reticence of "Reverie"—is the rivalry with Wagner as
flagrant, even if only by reason of a very calculated use of the term
"tetralogy." Several years earlier, at least, in *Sketched at the Theater*
("Genre or On Moderns"), the word appeared when Mallarmé

took up and redirected the critique that Gautier had leveled at the modern *théâtre du boulevard*, the vaudeville—at entertainment, that is. The "scene" was already set:

> Put before the immediate and forced triumph of the monster or Mediocrity that paraded in the divine site, I love Gautier applying to his tired gaze the black opera glass like a voluntary blindness and "It is an art so gross ... so abject," he explains, before the curtain; but as it in no way pertains to him, because of disgust, to annul his prerogatives of seer, it was, even more ironic, the sentence: "There should only be one Vaudeville—one would make a few changes from time to time." Replace Vaudeville by Mystery, or even by a multiple tetralogy itself being deployed parallel to a cycle of years begun over, and hold that its text be incorruptible as the law: there it is almost! (p. 313)

Yet it is the same word, "tetralogy," that returns in "Catholicism" when defining, under the names of "play" or "mass," a "Mystery, other than representational . . . , Greek." Thus when it appears that the model of tragedy does not suffice in the modern age:

> Here, recognize, from now on, in the drama, the Passion, to enlarge the canonical acceptation or, as this was the ostentatious aesthetic of the Church, with the beacon of hymns, a human assimilation to the tetralogy of the Year. (p. 393)

Of little importance here are the precise modalities of the public ceremonial that Mallarmé had in view and to which he often alludes. The decisive thing here is simply that the mass is tragedy, *without the stage*. And by this authority it is the latest model. Without doubt it presupposes the commemoration of a *drama* (the Passion) and consequently, to speak as Aristotle does, a certain *sustasis tôn pragmatôn*. But the drama (the Passion) is not represented, notwithstanding that Mallarmé enlarges upon "the canonical meaning" (the Mystery is precisely not a *mystery* in the medieval sense of the term). It must be *evoked*, that is to say also, as we will see, phrased and proffered. And as the Mallarméan mass is not, ultimately, Christian, it would retain the essential of the "fastuous aesthetic of the Church" (as "The Same" says: "Nonetheless, let us penetrate into the church, with art"); the drama is a drama of no one, or—Mallarmé continually turns to the word *aucun*—anyone (*aliquis unus*). It is thus a drama of death itself, of the "nothingness" of everyone. Or rather of this *intersection*—the term has its resources, which Mallarmé is not unaware of—where, for our "race" at least, god and man enigmatically separate and resemble each other simultaneously. That is to say, as long as memory is preserved in Christianity, the man-god is revealed, the "type" of Christ. The very intersection of the Passion.[14] After announcing that "Simply, in the inaptitude of people to perceive their nothingness if not as a hunger, profane poverty, apart from the accompaniment of the absolute thundering of the organs of death," "Catholicism" proposes this extraordinary formula, ultimately so close, it must be noted, to Hegel's meditation on the "hard word" of Luther's canticle "God himself is dead," and on the speculative reach of incarnation, in the chapter entitled "Religion Sublated" in *Phenomenology of Spirit*. With the exception that the absolute—which, Mallarmé alone, mixing coquetry and irony, recognized as his competence[15]—does not "want" "to be close to us" but is *afraid* of its very absoluteness. And with this other exception—Catholicism *oblige*—that the flesh is also the "entrails" and that the mystery is as much in conception as in suffering and death, on the side of what Mallarmé calls "the Mother":

> A race, ours, that has this honor of lending the entrails to the fear that has, itself, other than as human consciousness, the metaphysical and monastic eternity, comes to term, then of snuffing out the abyss with some harsh cry in the ages . . . (p. 391)

It is the kind of intuition that must not be allowed to be lost in an amnesia of origins, and whose tradition, on the contrary, must be maintained as firmly as possible. The fortune of art—of religion—lies entirely there. And because Christianity (Catholicism) is historically exhausted, because the Church visibly fails in its task—as does, on the other hand, the theater—we have to hope for a strictly political or civic (national) sort of sublation, even if we must for that at least provisionally renounce the "arduous zeal" and the ancient "sublimity." There must then be a fall, and a certain leveling. Several lines below, Mallarmé adds:

> [S]ummarily the Divinity, who is never but Oneself, is a matter of where transports felled by prayers mounted with the ignorance of the precious secret to measure its arc—at the level, to take it [Divinity] up again, as a point of departure, humble foundations of the city, faith in each one. This outline by assembly and a height like the sidewalk, there descends the quotidian gleam of the reverberation, within reach.
>
> Unknowing worship and the common functioning, as to the virtues, presented by a nation: before everything else [comes] the harangue that the flat ground exists following mutual piety—from there, the soul is free to be exiled on high. (p. 391)

From there it seems to be justified that Mallarmé retains from the mass only the "aesthetic" or the "art," the "beacon of hymns." That is to say, for the essential, music. But these hymns, this music that Mallarmé dreams of, requires a "crowd"—even, we might say, a community. I will return to this idea. Such that with art, it is equally a rite that is retained, a worship—the term "cult" [*culte*] is so to speak constant. And thus, all the same ("from there, the soul is free to be exiled on high"), the hope of a manner of revelation and, a strong word, of the arrival of *joy*: "Nonetheless let us penetrate into the church, with art: and if, we know it! the fulguration of ancient songs consumed the shade and illuminated such divination long since veiled, suddenly lucid and in rapport with a joy to install" (p. 395).

The mass is theater without spectacle, not conceding a stage, and consequently without spectators. The mass, neglecting "all the flattening whispered by the doctrine" and holding "to the solutions that the liturgical outburst proclaims," requires *participants*, even if they are only simple "auditors." The disappearance of the stage equals the presence, quasi-exclusive, of music. Whose great power, Mallarmé often repeats, is in all kinds of ways to touch the soul, even if, ultimately, it does not do so as immediately as language or, more precisely, verse.[16] As soon as there is music, there is mystery—and the promise of an initiation. Whence it is not only the auditor who must be substituted for the spectator; but this au-

ditor himself, the "amateur" (or "aesthetician," as an earlier version of the "Reverie" said), must in turn cede his place to the "par-
ticipant," one who is never, in any case, just a "spectator." We are
again "in church":

> Always that, in the place, a mystery is given: to what degree does one
> remain its spectator, or does one presume to have in it a role? I omit
> all the flattening whispered by the doctrine and hold to the solutions
> that the liturgical outburst proclaims: not that I listen as an amateur,
> perhaps careful, except to admire how, in the succession of these de-
> fenses, prose or motets, the voice, that of the child and of the man,
> disjointed, married, naked, or exempt from accompaniment other
> than the touch of a clavier setting the intonation, evokes to the soul
> the existence of a personality multiple and single, mysterious and
> nothing but pure. (p. 395)

This evocation to the soul—two words that are, again, as points of
condensation for the Mallarméan lexicon—of the "existence of a
personality multiple and single," indissociably the crowd and god,
and the one as the other in the enigma of the "there is" that music
brings on, such is what constitutes the mass as the model of "festi-
vals," "pomp" or "fasti" of the future. The mass is a ritual of participation, *metexis*, even of *partage* in the sense in which Jean-Luc
Nancy uses the word.[17] Moreover, Mallarmé himself, distancing
himself from the anthropo-theophagy latent in Roman Catholic
worship, does not hesitate to redeem communion, including the
Eucharist and the "real presence," which certainly are no longer
those of the Christian god-man but still could well be so through
what is instituted (and celebrated) as the being-in-common. Participation, for Mallarmé, is not ordered by any kind of identification that would authorize, as in the theater, the "representational
scission": it is properly *communal.*

> Our communion or share from one to all and from all to one, thus,
> derived from the barbarous meal that the sacrament designates—in
> the consecration of the host, nonetheless, the Mass, prototype of cer-
> emonials, despite the difference with a tradition of art, is affirmed.
> The amateur that one is, now, of something that ultimately is, would
> not know how to attend, as a passerby, a tragedy, even if it included

an allegorical return to him; and from close up, requires a fact—at least the credulity of this fact in the name of results. "Real presence": or, that the god be there, diffuse, total, mimed from afar by the actor erased, known by us trembling, by reason of all glory, latent although so excessive, that he assumed, then renders, struck by the authenticity of words and triumphal light, of Fatherland, or of Honor, of Peace. (p. 394)

Thus, a non-Christian communion. Or rather, a post-Christian one: Mallarmé foresees a certain "parity" between "liturgical reminiscences exclusively our own or original good" and "certain pageantry, profane, avowed." It is certainly not a question of envisioning some "lay" or "republican" ceremony, as was said at the time (to my knowledge, the word "Republic" never appears, and no mention is made of the diverse attempts at "revolutionary worship"): "A pretension that prides itself on its laicity except that this word invites a sense linked to the refusal of superior inspirations."[18] But neither is it a question of going back to the Christian rite pure and simple: "All is interrupted, effective in history: little transfusion." Something different will happen, following the anamnesis of a tradition (an origin), that is to say, also, a forgetting:

> Let us forget—
>   A magnificence will be deployed, something, analogue to the Shadow of the past. (p. 394)

And this is what Mallarmé sees, perhaps from far away, when toward the end of "The Same" he evokes the new theater of Trocadéro:

> The first hall that the Crowd possesses, at the Palais du Trocadéro, but interesting with the stage reduced to the floor space of the platform (the floorboards and the front of the chorus), its considerable buffet of organs and the public jubilating in being there, in an edifice undeniably devoted to festivals, implies a vision of the future: however, some of its traits were borrowed from the church, unknowingly. The representation, or the mass, is lacking: two terms, between which, at the desired distance, the pomp will hesitate. When the old religious vice, so glorious, of diverting natural feelings toward the in-

comprehensible, to confer upon them a somber grandeur, will be diluted in the waves of prominence and daylight, it will not remain less than, for example, devotion to the Fatherland, if it must find a sanction other than on the battlefield, in some joy, demands some worship: being that of piety. (pp. 396–97)

"A magnificence will be deployed, something, analogue to the Shadow of the past."

Analogue in what way?

When Mallarmé, again in the same text, describes the mass in its three elements ("Follow, three elements; they lead into each other"), two of these elements, the last two, form a quasi-theater, *with* music. A *quasi*-theater, because the priest, whose officiating gestures distance and withdraw the god in the very movement by which they were dedicated to designate him (as "Catholicism" says: "the god . . . mimed from afar, by the actor erased") is not an actor and (re)presents nothing and no one: "Although the priest herein has not the title of the actor, but officiates—designates and withdraws the mythic presence that one comes to merge with; far from obstructing it by the same intermediary as the actor, who stops thought with his cumbersome character." With music, one could imagine, because the organ, "relegated to the stops" (he is still at the Trocadéro), brings into the church the terrifying infinity of the pure outside, whose exteriority it annuls at the same time—and which it protects: "I will finish with the organ, relegated to the stops; it expresses the outside, an enormous stuttering of shades, or their exclusion from the refuge, before they overflow ecstatically and pacified, thus deepening it with the entire universe and causing the hosts the fullness of pride and security" ("The Same," p. 396). Which all the same sketches the quite clear contours of an economy of catharsis.

But in reality effective music is that which emanates from the participants themselves. And it is there that communion is produced:

> The nave with a crowd—I am not talking about spectators but about the elected: whoever can there throw to the vaults from the most humble source of a throat the response in uncomprehended Latin,

but exulting, participates between everyone and himself in the sublimity coiling back toward the choir: because here is the miracle of
singing; one projects oneself, high as the cry goes. Tell if artifice, better prepared and for many, egalitarian, than this communion, above
all aesthetic, in the hero of the divine Drama.[19]

Communion, here that of song and—mystery *oblige*—the "un-
comprehended Latin"—is thus accomplished, or operated (Mallarmé is attached to the word), "in the hero of the Divine drama."
    And there, precisely, is the decisive point. And what Mallarmé,
with tenacity, opposes to Wagner and to the device—theatrical,
too theatrical—of the musical drama and of the "total work of
art." Because in the conflict with Wagner, beyond a doubt, Mallarmé breaks away; there is a *decision*, and not only reserve or reticence. From the "Reverie" of 1885 to the last texts, on this point,
the gesture is the same and of an absolute clarity throughout.
(Mallarmé visibly does not miss an occasion, while saluting the
"genius" of Wagner, to separate himself from an already fanatical
Wagnerism.) And each time the decision comes to affirm the imperious necessity of what Mallarmé calls, we have already encountered the word, "type," or sometimes also "figure"—even, as here,
"hero"—which he conceives as the condition of the very possibility of worship (of communion). It is he, the type, who is lacking in
Wagner, as in Greek tragedy: in all theater that orders itself, finally, around a stage, and that is consequently encumbered by
characters. And it is he whose invention we must credit Catholicism with, who ultimately decides, alone or nearly so, modernity.
In its legacy of the type, Christian worship harbors all worship—
all art—to come. For the French, in any case: "the conclusion pre-
vails: in fact, it was impossible that in a religion, even in its abandon since, the race did not put its private, unknown secret. The
hour suits, with the necessary detachment, to practice there the
digging, to exhume the ancient and magnificent intentions" ("The
Same," p. 397).
    When he finally draws out the "lesson" of the mass, Mallarmé
writes this, which lends itself to no confusion:

Such, in the authenticity of distinct fragments, the staging of the State religion, by no framework yet outmoded and which, following a triple work, direct invitation to the essence of the type (here the Christ), then invisibility of this one, finally enlarging of the place to infinity by vibrations, strangely satisfies a desire of modern philosophy and art. (p. 396)

～

What, consequently, is the type?

Under this rubric, I tried to indicate elsewhere,[20] the entire problematic of mimesis has been engaged since Plato—if, at any rate, we do not amputate it in the least from its indissociably pedagogical and political "aesthetic." Jacques Derrida, it is true, has shown to what point Mallarméan mimetology undoes, perverts, and destabilizes all possible philosophical protocols, from Plato to Hegel—from one dialectic to another that claims to be, itself, the last, the logical accomplishment of philosophizing itself—of the question of mimesis. This was the object of the first part of "The Double Session": a stupefying reading of Mallarmé's *Mimic* offered the fortune of the undecidable and delivered the law without law, the hyper-logic, of *écriture*.[21] But in becoming attentive to the political discourse of Mallarmé, I would even say: to a certain haunting of Mallarmé—and the *agôn* with Wagner, what is it, ultimately, other than politics or aesthetico-politics?—a question cannot help but arise: why this strange *stop*, repeated, constant, nearly obstinate, at worship (communion), the type, and—I will return to it—myth? Why, *on this point*, the surely elliptical but all the same systematic sketch of a political and philosophical theory of a "great art" that underlies a declared onto-typology, like all the modern reversals of Platonism issuing, in reality, from romanticism?[22] Why then, more generally, the residue of this idea (from Schelling, even the "young" Hegel, to Nietzsche and George, that is to say also to Jünger and the Heidegger of the 1930's): according to which it falls to art, in the age where transcendence fails and is undone, to recover its ancient destination and establish the type; or, if one prefers, the mythological figure, where humanity, or perhaps *a* humanity (a people, for example), could recognize itself and get hold of its essence and its constitutive characteristic, less by "identification" than under the direct effect—under the *impression* or *mark*—of the historial seal that is the type? Why still assign to art this "vocation" or this "mission" to have to *type* the humanity that comes, and for whom, from now on, the figures and examples willed by traditions and religions obviously will no longer suffice?

Consequently the question is: to what point does the thought of Mallarmé come from such an onto-typology?

And because those are the stakes of the debate with Wagner, we must take the time to follow the veritable deconstruction of the *Gesamtkunstwerk* that Mallarmé effects. And begin a little further back.

~

It is in the name of Mystery, undeniably, that Mallarmé at once criticizes, in a very severe way, the theater (at least the contemporary theater because he saves, to some extent, the classical French tragedies, producing "in a milieu nil or nearly so . . . something like our plastic morality," ["Genre or On Moderns," p. 319]) and salutes in Wagner, with an admiration that is not false, the re-enthroning of theater: the new and publicized will to ceremonial.

His critique of theater, and not only of the stage, is well known. However, it must not be misunderstood. Assuredly there exists in Mallarmé—it often takes the foreground—a relatively external critique of theater. A critique that one might almost call sociological: the theater is, under the appearance and the illusion of art, bourgeois triviality itself (to which, for example, the triumph of realism or naturalism attests) and the overvaluing of a mundane "comedy," where one pretends to "be amused" "in the absence of all functioning of majesty and ecstasy" (p. 314). It is the theater of "Ladies" and "Gentlemen": "a monster"; a "stupid" or false temple that culminates—and Mallarmé shares this distaste with Wagner—in opera. But underneath this complaint, which is as we see already political, is hidden another, more properly aesthetic. It touches on the materiality of the stage (the "staging"), as it drowns the ideality of the theater—a motif that becomes a kind of model.

It is the famous declaration apropos of *Hamlet* in *Sketched at the Theater*: "The work of Shakespeare is so well fashioned following the only theater of our mind, which is the prototype of the rest, that it now makes the best of its staging, or does without one, with indifference."[23] But it also touches, as we have been able to see in the example of Greek tragedy, on the incapacity of the drama to elevate itself to the height of allegory, of emblem, or of myth. And consequently of Idea. And such is ultimately what justifies, in Mallarmé's eyes, the superiority of the ballet: "An art holds the stage, historical with Drama; with the Ballet, otherwise, emblematic."[24] Here again, it is crucial not to misunderstand.

Mallarmé always said it: the ballet is the purest form of theater, that is to say the closest to the presentation of the Idea. "Sketched at the Theater," for example, recalls it in these terms:

> The ballet gives only a little: it is the imaginative genre. When a sign of the scattered general beauty isolates itself for the gaze, flower, wave, cloud, and jewel, etc., if for us, the exclusive means of knowing it consists in juxtaposing to it the aspect of our spiritual nudity so that it feels it analogue and adapts it for itself in some exquisite merging between it and this flying form—nothing but through the rite, there, announced by the idea, doesn't the dancer seem to be half the element involved, half humanity apt at being merged there, in the floating and the reverie? The operation, or poetry par excellence, and the theater. Immediately the ballet results allegorical.[25]

Allegory: this is what a fundamental Platonism here—even if it is "aestheticized" in a modern way (the "cult of the imagination") and even if it tolerates a theater (at the limit, it is true, of pure *theorein*)—imposes as the very modality of the (sensual) presentation of the image: art, consequently, in its Platonic-Hegelian definition.[26] Elsewhere, in "Ballets," Mallarmé evokes the human form, in the dance, as the "visual incorporation of the idea" (p. 306) and it is linked to the question of rhythm, which we will come to. Notwithstanding that the ballet never gives more than a sketch, a particularly furtive one, of the ideal theater. It presents, this is certain, the advantage of including music, which we know "mobilizes" the theatrical marvel and which consequently prepares the theatrical "beyond" of theater: "The musical accompaniment, dispenser of Mystery," says "Sketched at the Theater" (p. 297). But it also represents the inconvenience of requiring a real stage: "The dance alone, by the fact of its evolutions, with the mime seems to me to necessitate a real space, or the stage" ("Genre or On Moderns," p. 315). Yet this material space unarguably annoys ideality ("Strictly, a paper suffices to evoke every play: aided by multiple personality everyone is able to play it within, which is not the case when it is a matter of pirouettes," p. 315). And this annoyance, not less arguably, is the fact of theater itself, whose materiality signifies in the last analysis the alternation of the elements that compose it. The theater is fundamentally impure:

> Always the theater alters from a special or literary point of view the arts that it takes up: music not concurring there without losing in depth and some shadow, nor song, some solitary thunder, and properly speaking, one could not recognize in the Ballet the name of Dance; which is, if you like, hieroglyph.[27]

The immediate consequence: the ballet is not the dance, which in reality can only be understood imaginatively, beyond theater, as a pure text of which the dancer would be the semiotic operator:

> The unique imaginative training consists, at ordinary hours of frequentation in the sites of Dance without aiming at some preliminary, in patiently and passively wondering before each step, each attitude so strange, these *pointes* and *taquetés, allongés* or *ballons.* "What can this signify" or better, with inspiration, to read it. Certainly one will operate in full reverie, but adequate: vaporous, clear and ample, or restrained, such only as encloses her in its circuits or transports her by a fugue the unlettered ballerina delivering herself to the business of her profession. ("Ballets," p. 307)

A further consequence, but more decisive—beyond this infatuation of the age for the dance: it is not essentially through what it presents to the eye that the real theater can act. It is through the music that accompanies it, that is to say—let us not forget that music is Music, or "Muse-ic" [*Musaïque*][28]—through the "concurrence" of all the arts, poetry itself (the "literary principle") "sealing," for Mallarmé, this collaboration:

> Our only magnificence, the stage, to whom the concurrence of the diverse arts sealed by poetry attributes, from my point of view, some religious or official character, if one of these words has a meaning, I certify that the century finishing does not care about it, understood thus: and that this miraculous assembly of everything that is necessary for fashioning divinity, except for the clairvoyance of man, will be for nothing.[29]

From there comes the paradox that is the principle of the deconstruction of the *Gesamtkunstwerk*: there where we expect the critique of "too much theater" what we find is one of "too much music." It is not that Mystery, at whatever degree (of ideality), must remain in solidarity with a theater; nor that music, inversely, destroys the theater by submerging it. Very much to the contrary, as has been sufficiently argued. It is in reality that music, as an *organizing* principle, enters into competition with poetry. But not directly, as with Baudelaire, where it is simply a question of accomplishing lyricism. That is not at all the aim of Mallarmé, or is so only very tangentially. On the contrary, that the conjunction of music and the theater could make a claim to the Work, and above all produce such an *effect*, this is what worries Mallarmé and raises in him a suspicion: such that music in fact only has this incomparable power—this "magic"—inasmuch as it is linked to some theater, that it does not act alone. It is not music alone—even less music "itself"—that is involved. It is music inasmuch as it comes to underscore theatrical practice and assure, from right there, what the theater has always announced as its end: participation or communion. The deconstruction of the *Gesamtkunstwerk* proceeds from this intuition: not that music lends itself to theater, but that it is, by itself, already theatrical—that is to say producing, in its own way—a *fiction*. Music, in other words, is the great weakness of Wagner inasmuch as it comes from *musica ficta*. Which can also be understood: inasmuch as *musica ficta* is incapable of the figure or the type.

～

This deconstruction begins, by necessity, with the *reconstruction* of the Wagnerian project. A reconstruction that is critical, in some sense, but in no way hostile. Vis-à-vis Wagner, regardless of the gravity of the conflict, Mallarmé's tone is reserved. Measured, even. And thus, again, admiring. There is an extraordinarily Mallarméan probity.

For example, not for one instant does Mallarmé challenge the "genius" of Wagner ("genius" is even probably the word that comes up most frequently about Wagner, and it is completely serious). And there where the political stakes, that is to say in the national sense, are the most directly involved, Mallarmé does not cede. In 1886, he raised an extremely virulent protestation against the cabal set up by the French public—and, it seems, encouraged by the authorities—on the occasion of a performance of *Lohengrin* at the Eden (which is, because of its ballets, the theater par excellence for Mallarmé): "What stupidity and notably in the political sense invading everything, so much that I speak of it! to have lost an elementary occasion . . . to manifest to a hostile nation the courtesy that undoes the surly event; when it was a question of saluting Genius in its blinding glory." An exacerbated protestation, almost as radical (and desperate) as that of Rimbaud in 1871: without a doubt, it does not invite desertion or "collaboration" with the Prussians against the shamed Versaillais; all the same, it evokes an exile, simultaneously aesthetic and political: "It is in fleeing the fatherland that from now on it will be necessary to satisfy our soul beautifully." "Everyone, again here we are, who seeks a form of worship with art in relation to time . . . , is obliged to take materially the path of the foreigner, which is endured not without displeasure, by the simple instinct of the artist, to leave the soil of the country" ("Parenthesis," pp. 323–24). And do we see to what point that sounds like Hölderlin, at the dawn of the year 1800? or that the feeling of guilt is the same as that of Baudelaire in 1860?

There is here, the evidence suggests, a whole national scene, which, above all, we must not underestimate. But, on Mallarmé's part, no ulterior motive: behind his reticence toward Wagner, severe but delicate (extremely polite), lies a recognition that cedes nothing to that of Baudelaire. The clearest text in this regard is the conclusion of the "Reverie":

> Here is why, the Genius! me, the humble one serving an eternal logic, oh Wagner, I suffer and reproach myself, in the minutes marked by solitude, not to number with those who, annoyed by everything in order to find the definitive salvation, go straight to the edifice of your Art, for them the term of the path. It opens, this incontestable gateway, in these times of jubilee that are for no one people, hospitality against the insufficiency of self and the mediocrity of fatherlands; it exalts those fervent to the point of certitude: for them it is not the greatest course ever ordered by a human sign that they run with you, as conductor, but the finite voyage of humanity toward an Ideal.[30]

It is not only that the "me, the humble one serving an eternal logic" is opposed to a "Genius" as the claimed French clarity is opposed to the no less claimed German depth. The "eternal logic" here is logic as such, and the "French spirit" was defined shortly before as "strictly imaginative and abstract, thus poetic" (p. 544). And I return to the fact that here it is a question of the very conception of poetry, that is to say, of art. What Mallarmé cannot, in reality, subscribe to—an offer he declines—is the idea or the belief that Wagnerian art, "accomplishing" art, would offer the "definitive salvation." Mallarmé does not allow himself to be carried off, nor, above all, seduced: he is reluctant—the "ideological" resistance is patent—before the "certitude" of the "fervent." Who not only throw themselves into running, with Wagner as their guide (what reticence, before the fact, to the *Führung*!), a course in fact recognized as "the greatest ever ordered by a human sign," but also are persuaded that they accomplish "the finite voyage of humanity toward an Ideal." The text first of all aims at "European" Wagnerism, that is to say the supranational illusion (beyond the "mediocrity of fatherlands") of an accomplishment of humanity according to art, in the communal space of a festival (a "jubilee") where the differences between peoples are erased.

Thus, recognition *and* reserve. In this conjunction lies the whole national question. For Mallarmé, it is a fact: all art is national. Even if all the nations are not, to an equal extent, capable of art "in its integrity," says Mallarmé, which means: inasmuch as it is really *poetic*, or creative.[31] If, as a result, Mallarmé cannot adhere to Wagnerism, beyond his repugnance toward all kinds of unanism, it is evidently because of mistrust of a national art (and of the art of this particular nation, Germany) that claims universality. First of all, for the reason that such a pretension demands an act of faith: Mallarmé does not call it "eternal logic" lightly. But also for the reason that this way of carrying off the adherents, through the intermediary of fervor, implies a scarcely developed idea of art and, as a consequence, means that are both too gross and too primitive. Inasmuch as he wants to found a national art, Wagner returns to origins, or to what he understands as origins. These are only beginnings, replies Mallarmé, who does not allow us to confuse myth with legend or the original with the antique. And who wants not a foundation but a celebration. In the pro-Wagner protest of 1886—in the text of "Parentheses," "these light Notes taken aside in a corner and nevermind when in the background vibration of an evening"—the sentence was nevertheless quite severe: " . . . an art, the most comprehensive of this time, such that by the omnipotence of a total and archaic genius it fails and forever at the beginning of a race our rival" (p. 323).

That is why Mallarmé does not disapprove of the Wagnerian project. In any case, he approves its critical aspect. For example, on the subject of the poverty and grossness of a theater founded on the simple demand of belief—that is to say, ordered, for the needs of participation (of identification)—by the dramatic presence of the character:

> Doubts and necessities, for a judgment, to discern the circumstances that will meet, at the beginning, the effort of the Master. He emerges at the time of a theater, the only one that can be called decrepit, so much its Fiction is fabricated of an uncouth element: because it is imposed evenly and all at once, commanding belief in the existence of a person and of adventure—belief, simply, nothing more. ("Reverie," p. 542)

Yet Mallarmé knows well—he is himself the first to feel—that "the Modern disdains imagining" and that he expects that in the concurrence of all the arts, "each will take it to the point where the power of illusion will manifest itself." And if he will "consent" only at this price, it is because the ancient code of belief—that is to say, illusion—has crumbled:

> It was really necessary, that the Theater before music took off from an authoritarian and naive concept, when its masterpieces were not using this new resource of evocation, alas! lying in the pious pages of the book, without the hope, for anyone, of spilling over into our solemnities. Its play remains inherent to the past, or so a popular representation would repudiate it, because of this intellectual despotism: the crowd wanting in it, following the suggestion of the arts, to be mistress of its credence. (p. 542)

Mallarmé thus does not contest for one moment the "attachment" of music, nor anyway its power of "mobilization," that is to say its magic in the strongest sense of the term. He would know quite well that this "enchantment" or this "charm" that has no other end than to restore the conditions of illusion and adhesion is the very danger of music. Nietzsche, at the same time, and for the same reasons (in the name, in any case, of a siege on illusion), spoke of the *virtus dormitiva* of music. With Mallarmé, we are almost at hypnotism:

> As if this faith demanded of the spectator need not precisely result from what he draws from the concurrence of all the arts inciting the miracle, otherwise inert and nil, of the stage! You have to submit to a charm, for the accomplishing of which it is not too much for any means of enchantment implicated by musical magic, in order to shake up your reason captured by the simulacrum, and emblematically one proclaims: "Suppose that that really takes place and that you are there!" (p. 542)

This does not prevent music from being what makes the theater move from drama (and its "cumbersome characters") to allegory. Assuredly. Yet we hear some reserve coming out:

> A simple orchestral attachment changes entirely, annulling its very principle, the former theater, and it is as strictly allegorical, that the scenic act now, empty and abstract in itself, impersonal, has need, to

start moving with verisimilitude, of the use of the vivifying emanation that Music spreads. (p. 542)

We hear some reserve coming out because we understand very quickly that in Mallarmé's eyes music cannot be attached, so simply (or "like that") to the theater. If it were so, that would never result in anything but opera or melodrama, for which Mallarmé, like Wagner, has the greatest scorn. It is clear that if the introduction of music "changes entirely" and annuls in its "principle" the "former theater," this is because it suppresses the drama—and *mimesis*, or what was called "the effect of the real" [*l'effet du réel*] a few years ago. Stripped of its only support of speech—and mimicry—the theater can no longer content itself with "recounting." Music forces it to say something else, that is, to *allegorize*. From there, the stage becomes an abstract place, the scenic act gives access to impersonality. Or, if we prefer, the character disappears to the advantage of the *figure*. The death of imitation is the life of the theater, but only music, in the sense in which it is "ideal," can incite or assure this life:

> Its presence! nothing more, of Music, is a triumph, for barely does it apply itself at all, even as their sublime aggrandizement, of antique conditions, but bursts out the generator of all vitality: an auditor will feel this impression that, if the orchestra ceased to spill out its influence, the mime would become, immediately, a statue. (pp. 542–43)

Yet this musical resurrection of the theater—this renaissance, Nietzsche would have said—implies that in fact, in its "principle," the former theater is destroyed, the one that knew nothing of "orchestral attachment": "the Musician and close confidant of his art, can he simplify its attribution just to this essential aim?" Apparently not:

> Him, he does this.
>   Going to the most urgent, he conciliated a whole tradition, intact, soon to be in disuse, with what of the virgin and the occult he guessed how to meld, in his partitions. Beyond a perspicacity or sterile suicide, so vivaciously abundant the strange gift of assimilation in this creator, however, that of the two elements of beauty that exclude each

other and, at least, are unaware of each other, personal drama and ideal music, it effected a hymen. Yes, with the aid of a harmonious compromise, inciting an exact phase of theater, which responds, as by surprise, to the disposition of its race. (p. 543)

The tone is barely polite ("the strange gift of assimilation in this creator, however"), and the complaints are visibly numerous.

Wagner, first of all, has not touched theater. He kept "intact" the tradition, a moribund tradition: "soon to be in disuse." The gesture is without radicality, it is a gesture of compromise: an effort of conciliation between the old theater and "the virgin and the occult"—thus, what is properly *modern*, "he guessed how to meld, in his partitions." The dramaturge in Wagner was not at the level of the musician. But what is serious here is that the compromise—the "hymen"—is between "two elements of beauty that exclude each other and, at least, are unaware of each other": drama and music. It is in its very principle that the *musical drama* is decrepit: it is nothing but opera—and Mallarmé, ultimately, does nothing but turn against Wagner the Wagnerian critique of opera. Far from annulling theater, as a fictional machination in any case, music reinforces it. And reinforces it simply, which is worse, to respond to the "disposition" of the German people. The innovation, if there is any innovation, is only national.

Certainly, the compromise is well done:

The tact is prodigious that, without totally transforming any of it, operates, on the stage and in the symphony, the fusion of these disparate forms of pleasure. (p. 543)

But it is nothing but a compromise. And, as such—a new aggravating circumstance—because it does not touch the theater, it is the music that is affected. Wagner's music is music, but not *the* music. Or it is a music forgetful of its own "principle"—an irreparable defect, in Mallarmé's eyes:

Even though philosophically it does nothing there but is juxtaposed, Music (I summarize that one insinuates where it points to, its first meaning and its fatality) penetrates and envelopes Drama by awe-inspiring will and allies itself to it: no ingenuity or profundity as with an enthusiastic awakening does it produce in this design, except that its very principle escapes Music. (p. 543)

Consequence: the Wagnerian drama does nothing but repeat, in a mode that is particular to Germany (that is to say, familiar to the German public), Greek tragedy, which we know for Mallarmé is only an insufficient model of Theater (of Mystery). The music of Wagner is subordinated to the drama: it serves only to signify, or illustrate, the character. It does not exist for itself. It is a "stage music" with a diffuse remainder ("floating," says Mallarmé, using the same word as Nietzsche). Its rule is, unfortunately, the *Leitmotiv*:

> Now, in fact, a music that has of this art only the observance of very complex laws, only first of all the floating and the infused, merges colors and lines of the character with the timbres and themes in a richer ambiance of Reverie than any air from here below, deity costumed in the invisible folds of a tissue of chords. (pp. 543–44)

In other words, Wagner is content with wrapping a character in music. Music is drapery. And as its aptitude for signification is nevertheless quite weak, and its narrative capacity practically nil, it has definitively the function of a signal. Not only is it redundant in respect to action (the drama); it also announces. In sum, it offers directions for the use of *representation*. Such is the reason why Wagner does not touch the theater. But such is the reason, above all, why he must have recourse to myth, or more exactly, to legend (the word that Baudelaire thought flattering, Mallarmé reverses the value of). Legend is what permits theater, aided by the "orchestral attachment," to "profit from familiars beyond the human individual." It thus marks the articulation, in a very precise way, between music (subordinated) and the theater (unchanged): "Here on the stage is Legend enthroned." The *musica ficta* becomes music-fiction, a pure heroic moiré that, attempting to represent the human, suggests only the faraway. From simple beginnings:

> Always the hero, who treads on fog as much as our soil, will be revealed in a faraway that the vapor of pleas, glories, and the joy emitted

by instrumentation fills, withdrawn thus at the beginnings. He acts only surrounded, in the Greek way, by the mixed stupor of intimacy that a public feels before the myths that have almost never been, so much their instinctive past melts! without however ceasing to profit from its familiars beyond the human individual. Some even satisfy the spirit by this fact of not seeming deprived of any acquaintance with symbols of chance.

Here on the stage is Legend enthroned.

With a former piety, a public, for the second time, first Hellenic, now German, considers the secret, represented, of origins. Some singular good fortune, new and barbarous, seats it: before the moving veil, the subtlety of orchestration, to a magnificence that decorates its genesis. (p. 544)

However, as Mallarmé immediately adds, decidedly severely (it is necessary to reread all this quite slowly and weigh each word): "It is all dipping into the primitive stream: not back at its source." Wagnerian theater returns, of course, to origins—to the primitive, the archaic. But this is precisely why it does not reach the origin. No more than Greek tragedy, of which it is the weak repetition. It is an art that is ultimately not *modern*, as all art ought to be from now on, in that it does not interrogate its own possibility of existence—from the example of the act of writing, in France, scrutinizing itself "all the way to the origin."[32] It is nothing but theater. Yet the Theater is something else entirely.

Mallarmé's response in an interview:

I believe that literature, taken up at its source, which is Art and Science, will furnish us a Theater, whose performances will be the true modern worship; a Volume, explanation of man, sufficient to our most beautiful dreams. I believe all that written in nature in such a way as not to allow any to close their eyes but those interested in seeing nothing. This work exists, everybody has attempted it without knowing it. To show that and raise a corner of the veil of what might be such a poem, is in isolation my pleasure and my torture.[33]

The Theater is literature itself, Volume or Poem. That of which Wagner did not have the least idea. If you prefer: the Theater, in its truth, is not theatrical. It does not have to submit itself to the imperatives of performance, with what that presupposes not only about the materiality of the stage (decor, costumes, etc.), but also of the technique of illusion, of the machination necessary to incite participation. From there it follows that the veritable theater has no need of music, "in the ordinary acceptation" as *Music and Letters* says. And the veritable music in no way has as its function to "accompany." Theater, if that means performance, simultaneously engulfs music and poetry. That is to say, practically all of art.

Whence comes the appeal to the "French spirit," which is "strictly imaginative and abstract, thus poetic," and which has no need of legend "on this point in accord with Art in its integrity." Inasmuch as in its essence it is an invention, the veritable art excludes everything out of date. It must be resolutely—or absolutely—modern. And thus not allow itself to lean toward mythology:

> See them, not keeping from days gone by any enormous primitive anecdote, like a prescience of the anachronism it would bring into a theatrical performance, Ritual of one of the acts of Civilization. Unless Fable, virgin of all place, time, and person known, is unveiled, borrowed from the meaning latent in the concurrence of everyone, that [Fable] inscribed on the page of the Heavens and of which History itself is only the vain interpretation, that is to say a Poem, the Ode. What! the century or our country, which exalts it, has dissolved Myths by thought, to remake them! The Theater calls them, no: not fixed, nor secular and notorious, but one detached from personality, because it composes our multiple aspect: that, with prestige corresponding to the national functioning, Art evokes, to mirror it in us.[34]

This refusal of legend—of myth—is evidently made in the name of a pure Fable or pure Myth, in the original sense of *fari* or *mythéomai*. "Pure" means, it is explicit: "virgin of all place, time, and person known." Not the least "anecdote" then, old or not; no hero, no geographic or historic references. This Speech is exclusively of the unknown, that is to say of this, we remember, that human beings exist and consequently so does a god (or a transcendence): Fable "borrowed from the meaning latent in the concurrence of everyone, that inscribed on the page of the Heavens." It is the poem or the song ("the Ode") taken absolutely. One could almost speak of a *transcendental* Fable, an inscription prior to everything that happens ("of which History itself is only the interpretation"). Or rather: (empty: "vain")[35] inscription of this: that *it happens*, that is to say, first of all, that there is language (and thus "national functioning"). Fable is Speech *a priori*.

No mythology, no "history" (even less plot), no characters. In consequence, no "theater." And yet a *presentation*, that of the Type or the Figure ("the Figure that No one is"): the pure presentation of a pure figure. And thus, it is necessary to believe, a pure theater. Let us call it a *theory*. It is the Mystery, a Mass itself pure. The Type, in that it is not anybody, would have for its function to "sum up" (symbolically or allegorically) "our dreams of places or of paradise," that is to say our dreams of the accomplishment, here or beyond, of the human. The Type would *represent* the essence and the destiny of humans—the "spiritual fact," as Mallarmé says. Here is the Theory of the Type:

> Type without prior denomination, for the surprise to emanate: his gesture sums up around him our dreams of places or of paradise, which the ancient stage engulfs with an empty pretension to contain them or to paint them. Him, someone! neither this stage, somewhere (the connected error, stable decor and real actor, of the Theater missing Music): is it that a spiritual fact, the full development of symbols or their preparation, necessitates a place, in which to develop itself, other than the fictive foyer of vision darted by the gaze of a crowd! Holy of holies, but mental . . . then arrives there, in some supreme flash, from which is awakened the Figure that No one is, each mimed attitude taken by it [the Figure] from a rhythm included in the symphony, and delivering it! Thus come to expire as if at the feet of the incarnation, not without a certain bond linking them thus to his humanity, these rarefactions and these natural leaders that Music renders, background vibratory prolonging of everything like Life.
>
> Man, then his authentic terrestrial sojourn, exchange a reciprocity of proofs.
>
> Thus Mystery. ("Reverie," p. 545)

This general purification or, if one prefers, this reduction of everything to the pure state is in sum the *sublimation* of *mimesis*. In a sentence that has remained famous, Mallarmé proposed the relatively emphatic word "destruction." But the Mallarméan *operation* is less destruction than purification. Which destines art, brought back to the strictest sense and discharged from all function subaltern or foreign to its essence, to be what the entire Occident thought it should be: the *presentation*, not of a spiritual content, to speak like Hegel, but of *the* spiritual content itself, which is nothing other than the "mystery" of human existence. Be it the fact of language. This is also why this art can announce itself as the truth of religion—in particular of that in which is announced that *En arkhè èn ho logos*—and, *a fortiori*, of all the stories, myths, and legends immemorially held by humanity about its origins and the meaning of its existence.

But even from there, what I provisionally called the "deconstruction" of Wagner is not a deconstruction. Rather a reduction or a rarefaction, as if the only complaint against Wagner were, we can imagine it murmured in English: *too much*. And it is not a deconstruction because the very principle of (re)presentation is not touched. It is time to reread in full, or nearly, the page that, eight years after the "Reverie," Mallarmé again devoted to Wagner:

> Everything, the magnificent instrumental polyphony, the living gesture or the voices of characters and gods, with the surplus of excess brought to the material stage setting, we consider it, in the triumph of genius, with Wagner, awestruck by such a cohesion, or an art, that today becomes poetry: yet will it be that the traditional writer of verse, he who holds himself to the humble and sacred sacrifices of the word, attempts, following his unique resource subtly chosen, to rival! Yes, as an opera without accompaniment or song, but spoken: now the book will try to suffice, to open the interior stage and whisper its echoes. A versified ensemble invites to an ideal representation. . . . A theater, inherent in the mind, whoever looked at nature with a certain eye carries it with himself, resumé of types and harmonies; so that the volume opening its parallel pages confronts them. The precarious collection of diverse inspiration, it is made of this; or by chance, which need not, and to understand the position taken, never [but] be simu-

lated. Symmetry, as it reigns in every edifice, the most vaporous, of vision and of dreams. The vain *jouissance* sought by the former Dreamer-king of Bavaria in a solitary presence in the stage deployments, here it is, separate from the baroque crowd less than its vacancy on the steps, touched by the means or to restore the text, naked, of the spectacle. With two pages and their verse, I supplement, then the accompaniment of everything myself, the world! or I perceive there, discrete, the drama. This modern tendency subtracted from all contingencies of representation, gross or even exquisite until now, the work par excellence or poetry. ("Floorboards and Folios," pp. 328–29)

The theater of Mallarmé, even reduced to the Volume, is still a theater. And this is how we explain that the political (or religious) project of such a "theater" is not fundamentally different from the Wagnerian project, at least in principle, that is to say considering the undeniable "differences" (national, political, ideological, etc.). Mallarmé, like practically his entire century, dreams of an authority of art, which would also be just as well its authorization. It is ultimately a dream of official art. It is true that in all strictness, Mallarmé never for one moment compromises on the principle of purification or sublimation. But pure presentation of a Type, himself pure, "abstract" (even "negative") presentation, as Kant said, the Ceremonial remains nonetheless the presentation of the Type:

> An audience, it celebrates itself, anonymous in the hero.
> All, like the functioning of festivals:
> a people witnesses its transfiguration in truth.
> Honor.
> Search, where it is, something similar—[36]

One question nevertheless remains: if it is such an onto-typology that supports the Mallarméan project, what is its consequence as to the conception of music? That is to say, one suspects, as to the question of the rapport between "Music and letters"? What music, what writing does such a "theater" imply? And what should we understand by "music"?

"Floorboards and Folios," just read, opposes to the musical drama an "opera without accompaniment or song, but spoken": a

pure, paradoxical object. This recalls, assuredly, that if it is necessary to take support from the theater that musical attachment
raised to the rank of Ceremonial, we cannot expect from Music—
or above all from a music submitted to the stage and thus per-
verted as music—that it could, all alone, assure the "cohesion" that
defines art or the art work. But does that signify as well that the
word (or the "literary principle") is the truth of music? Yes, in a
certain way; and that is what it is necessary to try to understand.

Spoken opera, Mallarmé indicates immediately, is the Volume:
"Now the Volume will try to suffice, to open the interior stage
and whisper its echoes. A versified ensemble invites to an ideal
representation." The Volume is thus, at first, of a theatrical essence. Or, more precisely, it uses theater. The logic of the supplement, or rather of supplementarity, that "Solemnity" exhibits in a
very clear fashion: "A book, in our hand, if it announces some august idea, supplements all theaters" (p. 334). If this is so, the Volume is pure representation: "What representation! The world adheres to it." Pure representation, that is to say a means of supple-
menting the world itself: "With two pages and their verse, I
supplement, then the accompaniment of everything myself, the
world! or I perceive there, discreet, the drama." And we see that
the logic of supplementarity is in this case the same as that of purification or of sublimation. That is why in reality the Volume is
not, in essence, theatrical. It is rather an *archi-theater*, and the origin of representation.

Why risk the word "archi-theater"?

We know, from the well-known doctrine, that the Volume for
Mallarmé is a "structure" (that is the word used in "Crisis of
Verse"). Thus defined, it implies the "elocutionary disappearance
of the poet." It is a work without subject, being probably itself, in
Mallarmé's eyes, the Subject as such, that is to say the absolute as
Subject—and I do not think that the reminder of the Hegelian
formula is out of place here. This explains, also, the scorn Mallarmé holds for subjective poetry, lyricism in the postromantic
sense. Yet—and this is not indifferent—the subjective, in its restrained meaning, is metaphorized by melody: "Every soul is a

melody, which it is a matter of re-knotting; and for that exist the flute and the viola of everyone." But "every soul," *Music and Letters* this time says, "is a rhythmic knot." And it is right there, in the passage from melody to rhythm, that the difference between the subject and the Subject is played out. Essentially, the Volume—the Subject—is rhythm: spacing and scansion, in a certain sense: "the One differing in himself" according to the adage of Heraclitus rediscovered at the dawn of German idealism. "Crisis of Verse" proposes this formulation:

> The pure work implies the elocutionary disappearance of the poet, who cedes his initiative to words, mobilized by the force of their inequality: they are illuminated by reciprocal reflections like a virtual trail of fire of jewels, replacing perceptible respiration by the former lyric breath or the personal enthusiastic direction of the sentence.
>
> An order of the book of verse appears innate or everywhere, eliminates chance; even more is it necessary, to omit the author; however, a fatal subject implies, among the pieces together, such harmony as to the place, in the volume, which corresponds. Susceptibility for the reason that the cry possesses an echo—motifs will be balanced out in the same way, considered, at a distance, neither the incoherent sublime nor this artificial unity, in the old days, measured in block in the book. Everything becomes suspended, fragmentary disposition with alternation and *vis-à-vis*, concurring in the total rhythm, which would be the poem silenced, with blanks; only translated, in a way, by each pendent. (pp. 366–67)

One could invoke a good number of other texts.[37] All speak of nearly the same conception of the Volume as a rhythmic *organon*. Yet rhythm is not only what allows the Volume to be absolute, by omission of the author, that is to say, if we like, as Subject without subject. (This is, for example, the very famous: "Depersonified, the volume, inasmuch as one is separated from it as author, does not demand the reader's approach. Such, know, between human accessories, it takes place by itself: fact, being. The buried meaning moves and uses, in chorus, folios" ["Reserved Action," p. 372].) But this rhythmic idea of the Volume is the very condition of its archi-theatrical "functioning." Because in reality rhythm is an

archi-music. If the Volume "supplements all theaters," it is that
verse supplements all musics. A long passage in "Solemnity" is
completely explicit in this regard:

> The metaphoric heaven spread out around the thunder of verse, arti-
> fice par excellence at the point of simulating little by little and of in-
> carnating the heroes (just in what must be noticed in order not to be
> bothered by their presence, a trait); this spiritually and magnificently
> illuminated depth of ecstasy, it is really the pure in ourselves carried
> by us, always, ready to surge at the chance that in existence or be-
> yond art always fails. Music, certainly, that the instrumentation of an
> orchestra tends to reproduce only and to fake. Admire, in its all-pow-
> erful simplicity or faith in the vulgar and superior means, the elocu-
> tion, then the metric that refines it to a last expression, as a mind,
> refugee with a few folios, defies the civilization neglecting to con-
> struct, so that they take place, the prodigious Auditorium and Stage of
> his dream. The absent mime and finales or preludes also by the wood-
> winds, the brass, and the strings, this mind, put beyond circum-
> stances, awaits the obligatory accompaniment of the arts or does with-
> out them. . . .
>
> The marvel of a high poem seems to me that, as here, conditions
> are born that authorize its visible deployment and interpretation, first
> it lends itself to it and ingenuously as needed only replaces everything
> as it is lacking. I imagine that the cause of assembling, henceforth, in
> view of the festivals inscribed into the human program, will not be the
> theater, limited or incapable all alone of responding to very subtle in-
> stincts, nor music also too fleeting not to disappoint the crowd; but
> merging into itself the vague and the brutal that these two isolate, the
> Ode, dramatized or wisely cut; these heroic scenes an ode with several
> voices. (pp. 334–35)

The archi-theatrical power of the Volume, we see, depends on
the capacity of verse, "artifice par excellence"[38] to produce a *mimesis* that one could call ideal. Or pure, even in its fulgerance, only
simulating (or incarnating) the "heroes," figures or types, in a
stroke. Verse abbreviates, and therefore purifies, drama. As if Mallarmé drew from Aristotle the completely surprising conclusion
that versification is the *katharsis* of *mimesis*. Yet it is this very capacity that Mallarmé designates as "music," by which he means, it

is still very clear, not only the "Muse-ic" but also a music (an "elocution" or metrical *lexis*) that music itself, "the instrumentation of an orchestra," is only a means to fake or reproduce. The Volume is thus of an archi-musical essence. That is why Mallarmé is always thinking of an Ode and defines poetry as song. That is also why, no matter what he can say about music's "vivifying" power, Mallarmé does not stop criticizing the recourse to instruments (or the concert),[39] and affirming that poetry is the accomplishing of music. "Crisis of Verse" gives a famous example of this:

> Certainly, I never sit in the tiers at concerts, without perceiving among the obscure sublimity such a draft of some one of the poems immanent in humanity or their original state, even more comprehensible when silenced and when, to determine its vast line, the composer feels this facility of suspending as far as the temptation to explain himself. With a writer's prejudice, doubtless impossible to uproot, I figure that nothing will remain without being offered; that we are there, precisely, seeking, before the breaking of the great literary rhythms . . . and their scattering in the close articulated frissons of instrumentation, an art of achieving the transposition, to the Volume, of the symphony or unilaterally to recover our advantage: because, it is not elementary sonorities by the brass, the strings, the woodwinds, undeniably, but the intellectual word at its apogee that must result, with plenitude and evidence, as the ensemble of the relations existing in all, Music. (pp. 367–68)

We find here again, in filigree, the reproach addressed to Wagner, and beyond him, to all music: "Music's very principle escapes us." Music, and not only the musician—and also not only because the instrumentation cripples it—does not explain itself: through the fault of ideality, it is incapable of auto-reflection. Which means, among other things, that the musician can never scrutinize his art "all the way to the origin" and forbids him the *modern* program par excellence (that is to say the romantic program, *stricto sensu*). But which also means not arriving except at the "draft" of the original poem. And from there even missing the essence of music: either "the ensemble of the relations existing in all," which only "the intellectual word"[40] can give access to or produce. Even if, in its turn, it is barely explained, we get a good glimpse of what a mathematical-ontological conception of music Mallarmé here sticks to. Whether it derives from Pythagoras and Plato or from Fabre d'Olivet matters very little.[41]

The essential is this affirmation of a "universal harmony" and that this universal harmony, what I am resigned to calling *archimusic*—be thought out through rhythm.[42]

From here, evidently, proceeds the theory of verse, which is nothing other, ultimately, than the *theory of literature* itself. Is it necessary to review this? Wagner, in all his monumental importance, is not the only horizon of Mallarmé. Another "monument" closes, but differently from Wagner, also opens up, liberates the horizon: it is Hugo, who, without doubt, having versified everything, has practically forbidden literature (as a result of which he is responsible for the famous "Crisis of Verse" and the no less famous "Verse has been tampered with")[43] but who, by the very fact of this imperious enterprise (as for himself, however, Mallarmé speaks of a "mysterious task"), revealed the secret, or the mystery—the encrypted truth: that verse—and by that Mallarmé means all enunciation with scansion or meter, in general—is the essence of literature:

> Hugo, in his mysterious task, rebuilt all of prose, philosophy, eloquence, history in verse, and, as he was verse personally, he practically confiscated from those who think, discourse, or narrate, the right to enunciation. A monument in this desert, with silence far away; in a crypt the divinity as well as an unconscious, majestic idea—the knowledge that the form called verse is simply itself literature; that there is verse as soon as diction is accented, rhythm as soon as style. Verse, I think, with respect expected that the giant who identified it with the tenacious and ever steadier hand of a blacksmith, would come to be missing; for, itself, to be broken. All of language, adjusted to meter, rediscovering in it its vital breaks, escapes, following a free disjunction into a thousand simple elements; and, as I will indicate, not without similitude to the multiplicity of the cries of an orchestration, which remains verbal. ("Crisis of Verse," pp. 360–61)

"The form called verse is simply itself literature." But verse itself comes to be broken—it becomes "free"—and we have the (verbal) equivalent of the symphony, of the "multiplicity of the cries of an orchestration." Versification is thus the restitution of Literature as archi-music—this archi-music of which music is itself only the imitation or the (too) sensual presentation, compared to "the marvel of transposing a fact of nature in its vibratory near-disappearance following the play of language" (p. 368). It is a question of accentuation in the enunciation or "diction" (in the *lexis*), and of rhythm, itself assimilated to style. And if we set aside the case of rhyme, which Mallarmé considers specific to French prosody and which he evidently considers important, we see that two criteria are here in play: a visual (or spatial) criterion and a (temporal) acoustic criterion, rhythm as such being, we must understand, the articulation of both:

> Whereas there was, with language reigning, at first to harmonize it according to its origin, so that an august sense was produced: in the Verse, dispensing, ordering the game of pages, master of the book. Either its integrality appears, visibly, among the margins and the blanks; or it is hidden, call it Prose, nonetheless it is it [Verse] if some secret pursuit of music remains, in the reserve of Discourse.[44]

For this reason, verse is absolutely essential to the poem: "That every poem composed otherwise than in view of obeying the old genius of verse, is not one . . ." ("Solemnity," p. 332). But if it is thus absolutely essential to the poem, and thus to Literature, it is that metrics itself is "absolute" (this is the very principle of what in Hölderlinian language one could call sobriety, so much does Mallarmé insist on its opposition to "enthusiasm" and to the "delirium common to lyrics"). Or—it makes no difference—it is that verse is the absolute sign:

> Thus launched on its own the principle that is only—Verse! draws no less than it releases for its full development . . . the thousand elements of beauty rushing together and ordering themselves in their essential value. Sign! in the central gulf of a spiritual impossibility that nothing be exclusively to everything, the divine numerator of our apotheosis, some supreme mold that does not exist as any object: but it borrows,

to burnish a seal, all scattered deposits, unknown and floating according to some richness, and to forge them. (p. 333)

Onto a lexicon that is still Baudelairean, despite the mathematical allusion ("the divine numerator of our apotheosis"), the lexicon of onto-typology comes to superimpose itself: the "supreme mold," the "seal," "to forge" (even "borrows" [*emprunte*], if we do not exclude that Mallarmé allows "imprint" [*empreinte*] to resonate in it). Yet, to make this definition of verse connect with the very famous description of "transposition" (the other decisive word, with "structure," to designate poetic work)—"I say: a flower! and, beyond the oblivion where my voice designs no shape, inasmuch as anything other than the calyxes we know, musically arises, the idea itself, suave, absent from all bouquets" ("Crisis of Verse," p. 368)— we see clearly that what orders the conception of archi-music (of Literature), is a fundamental onto-typology: verse (the sign) is only music insofar as it fashions or "fictions" the idea, that is to say, the thing itself in its essence (whence, also, the reiterated reference to the myth of Vulcan). Verse—art, absolutely—is the stamp of what is: character or Letter as that from which, in sum, because we add nothing to nature, there is a world. The Letter is the transcendental itself, and such is that which Mallarmé calls "Music." Which, as if Mallarmé remembered the archaic sense of the word, is essentially rhythm: seal, type, letter, character—scheme. That is why Mallarmé can speak of "the musicality of everything," which is the affair of the mind (*Music and Letters*, p. 645). And finally suspend his interrogation with this:

> Languages, imperfect in that several miss the supreme: thinking being writing without accessories, nor whispering but still tacit the immortal word, the diversity, on earth, of idioms prevents anyone from proffering the words that would, otherwise be found, by a unique mark, itself materially the truth. This express prohibition holds sway, in nature (we come up against it with a smile) that is no reason worthy to consider oneself God . . . —*Only*, that we know *the verse would not exist*: it remunerates philosophically the defect of languages, completely superior.

Strange mystery; and, from no lesser intentions, did metrics spring forth in incubatory times. ("Crisis of Verse," pp. 363–64)

Postscript

The review *fig.*, edited by Jean Daive, published in its fourth volume (December 1990) two unpublished pages of Mallarmé's "Volume," with a study by Eric Benoit ("Salutaris hostia") on the Ceremonial as envisioned by Mallarmé, and its relation to Catholic ritual. There is confirmed, in condensed form, the idea of religion (of art) that Mallarmé made for himself against Wagner—and the theology that supports it (God is the being of man, that is to say language). I will reproduce here, with the authorization of Jean Daive, these two passages:

> Le sauveur—nous
> le devenons tous— —
> faisons même chose—
> avec
> — —il manque
> l'office.
>
> consécrateur
> divine présence
> l'acteur devant
> rester invisible
> *il y est*
>
>
> The savior—we
> become him all— —
> let us do same thing—
> with
> — —lacking
> the mass
>
> consecrator
> divine presence
> the actor in front
> to remain invisible
> *he is there*

(It follows that the invisibility of the actor, the presentation without presentation of the Type, who is the "divine presence' [consecration], is the presentation of language itself as the possibility of all presentation. An absolute paradox that is the completion of sublimity: there art loses strength wanting to be *itself*—like religion.)

§3 Heidegger

> We are gathered together in commemoration of the composer
> Conradin Kreutzer, a native of our region. If we are to honor
> a man whose calling it is to be creative, we must, above all,
> duly honor his work. In the case of a musician this is done
> through the performance of his compositions.
> Conradin Kreutzer's compositions ring forth today in song
> and chorus, in opera and in chamber music. In these sounds
> the artist himself is present; for the master's presence *in the
> work* is the only true presence. The greater the master, the
> more completely his person vanishes behind his work.
> The musicians and singers who take part in today's cele-
> bration are a warrant that Conradin Kreutzer's work will
> come to be heard on this occasion.
> But does this alone constitute a memorial celebration? A
> memorial celebration [*Gedenkfeier*] means that we think back,
> that we *think* [*denken*]. Yet what are we to think and to say at
> a memorial which is devoted to a composer? Is it not the dis-
> tinction of music to "speak" through the sounding of tones
> and so not to need ordinary language, the language of words?
> And yet the question remains: Do playing and singing alone
> make our celebration a thoughtful celebration, one in which
> we think? Hardly! And so a "memorial address" has been put
> on the program. It is to help us think back both to the com-
> poser we honor and to his work.
>
> —Heidegger

With the exception of mathematical or mathematical-cosmo-
logical kinds of speculations, having, like those of Leibniz, an incontestable metaphysical capacity,[1] it would not be an exaggeration
to propose that, by most reckonings, nothing really has happened
in more than two thousand years between music and philosophy,
and that the history of their relations is, in a word, quite dull. Ultimately, the philosophers who have spoken of music are rare
(compared to the volume of discourse dedicated to the so-called
"plastic" arts, and, above all, to literature), and when they have
agreed to speak of it, as was necessary in the age of philosophy

where the ideal of the System required an aesthetic that was itself systematic, they have often done so in an obscure or borrowed manner, without knowing too well what to say or what to do with music, or where exactly to situate it (Kant illustrates this difficulty fairly well); or rather, inversely, but this is only the reverse, in an exalted manner. The two approaches are moreover able to cohabit perfectly, as the example of Schopenhauer demonstrates. Even Hegel does not seem entirely at ease. So that, as irritating annoyance or pathos, music has barely had any luck with philosophy, and one could easily suspect, especially today, that it is a question of the rebel object par excellence, rebelling against philosophy's takeover and perhaps, for this reason, continuously and silently indicating a limit to philosophy, a secret obstacle to its full deployment (to reasoning), even, possibly, a menace.

Yet in this story so lacking in highlights there are two events, one at the beginning and one (nearly) at the end of what today we can determine to be something like a properly so-called history of philosophy, both of which are violent events—brutal movements of rejection. With the inauguration of the ontologico-political project of philosophy, and simultaneous with the expulsion or exclusion from the City of the tragic poet-actor and the "myth-makers," came the expulsion of the quasi-totality of music (only military music was rigorously spared). And at the other end, and overdetermined by the no less ontologico-political project of a "reversal of Platonism," comes the rupture of Nietzsche with Wagner.

Taken by themselves, these two events, with their very strong symbolic charge (let us agree, for a moment, that they open and close the philosophical adventure, that they limit or delimit it: if this is so, philosophy would have constructed and deployed itself as an antimusic, and the emblematic "Socrates, make music!" would have remained a pious vow, that is to say, an indefinitely late repentance)—these two events, then, are completely enigmatic. And they are so in two ways.

A first time because they force an interrogation of the danger, seemingly incredible, that music would have represented in regard to—let us use Platonic terms—the exercise of right thinking and the healthy order of the being-in-community supporting itself by truth. What in music could have, or can, provoke such an aversion, even such a repulsion, and drive thought to such trenchant gestures?

A second time because, in the one as in the other case, it is a question of a pitiless agonistic scene—a typed and nearly exemplary or canonical scene of "mimetic rivalry"—with its most awaited effects, and particularly this: what is condemned and rejected (let us call it, as in Greek, Music: *hè mousikè* or *ta mousika*, Muse-ic, if you will)[2] inevitably returns: dialogue, for example, that is to say the dramatic or mimetic mode, in the writing of Plato (*The Laws*, we remember, are presented as the most beautiful of tragic poems), or the myth, in Plato but above all in Nietzsche, as word inclining to music—and I am thinking not of the "compositions" of Nietzsche but of the composition of *Zarathustra*. What, in music, was able to haunt to this extent the exercise of thought and, in the same movement, its fundamentally political preoccupation?

I do not have the intention here of describing or examining these two events in themselves; and the fact that I can thus relate one to the other does not in any way signify that I am confusing them or reducing the one to the other. It seems to me simply that the second is not foreign to the first, and that it is even a certain paradoxical and subtle form of repetition. But long analyses would be necessary to show this and unfold all of its consequences; and probably the question of music would not be central to it.[3] I will thus take a shorter path and reduce my intention to this: to attempt to seize the nature of *agôn* and consequently to understand what exactly, in the fact of music, is rejected by philosophy.

~

To enter into the question, and tighten the angle on the political stakes, which are explicit and recognized as essential, I will apply myself to the second of these events: the rupture of Nietzsche with Wagner, and I will take as my point of departure—political ontology *oblige*—one of the rare remarks by Heidegger on this subject. It is a matter of a very brief allusion, in an additional note to the lecture of 1938 called "The Age of the World Picture." There Heidegger criticizes the concept of value—it was, at the time, one of his frequent themes—and, in conclusion, approaches what he elsewhere calls Nietzsche's "going astray" in moral philosophy. Here is his presentation of things:

> Because Nietzsche's thinking remains imprisoned in value representation, he has to articulate what is essential for him in the form of a reversal, as the revaluation of all values. Only when we succeed in grasping Nietzsche's thinking independently of value representation do we come to a standing-ground from which the work of the last thinker of metaphysics becomes a task assigned to questioning, and Nietzsche's antagonism to Wagner becomes comprehensible as the necessary turning point of our history.[4]

The message is very clear. The code is far less so.

The message says, following the expectations and logic of the *Seinsgeschichte*, that phraseology—and "ideology"—of values, even in the figure of inversion or reversal, obfuscates the truth of Nietzsche's thought and bars access, for Nietzsche first of all, to its "fundamental metaphysical position": its determination of the Being of being as Will to Power and, at full term, as Will to Will. It is thus necessary to read Nietzsche "contra" himself (this is in outline the program of the five semesters of courses on Nietzsche, already well under way at the time)[5] and above all to interpret him "independently of the idea of value," this affliction of scholarly subphilosophy, which has not the least idea of what nihilism is in its terrifying gravity (which, itself, continually feeds on moral philosophy). Put another way, it is necessary to unburden Nietzsche of all that "reactive" part of his thinking in order to propose it, as the last (possible) thinking of metaphysics, for the task of questioning that touches on the History of Being, which is indissociably the questioning of history and the questioning of Being and the truth of Being (it was almost at the same time that Heidegger wrote that Being is nothing but the History of Being). Only on this condition could one perceive, in Nietzsche's rupture with Wagner, not *one* but *the* turning point—"the necessary turning point of our history"—even perhaps the turning point of History itself.

Such then, schematically outlined, is Heidegger's message, which also could not fail to be surprising in the era when it was made public (1949):[6] the conflict of Nietzsche and of Wagner, as the German text says forcefully (it does not say anything about "turning point"), could not be other than "the necessity of our History," an expression without the least equivocation if we do not mistake the value of the genitive, and if we understand clearly that the combat of Nietzsche contra Wagner is not a necessary consequence of History but a necessity for our History (and this is probably what the translator believed himself authorized to explicate, at the risk of introducing, in a context that perhaps does not tolerate it, a very heavy word from the Heideggerian lexicon).

But it is there that the code comes in and that, contrary to appearances, the message reveals itself to be not so clear.

In the code that was his during the entire national-socialist period, before but above all after the "retreat" in which Heidegger obstinately developed—in particular in his teaching on Nietzsche—his "differential explication" (his *Auseinandersetzung*) vis-à-vis Nazism, "our History" does not refer to the History of the European Occident and, consequently, to the *Seinsgeschichte*, the History of Being, inasmuch as "our History" is *first* about the History of Germany and of the German people, understood as place and language, the space or site of thinking—the *Da*—where the philosophical destiny of the entire Occident comes to be collected and completed, and to prepare for itself "another beginning" in the form of salvation—which, at this period, is conceived as the recommencing or the repetition (the *Wiederholung*) of the Greek commencement, which is and remains the send-off of such a destiny.[7] A fundamentally *political* preoccupation is not absent from such a determination, a word that Heidegger evidently would have dismissed, in its empirical usage in any case, but that is absolutely indispensable here. (Such is the logic of the "retreat": it retraces the very thing from which it removes itself.[8] A gulf could separate the thinking of the recommencement from the workings of the *Amt* Rosenberg; it does not prevent the former from insisting on declaring itself as the truth of the latter.)[9]

The *political* stakes of the interpretation of Nietzsche, then, are extremely clear: it is not only a question of showing the absolute coherence of Nietzsche's thought and its belonging, in its final phase, to the History of metaphysics. If Heidegger exhumes and recomposes Nietzsche's philosophy, on a scale without precedent, it is also a question of tearing Nietzsche away from the Nazi interpretation—that is, from the Nazi confiscation. That is to say, indissociably, from biologism (racist pseudo-biology) and from axiologism (axiomatic reasoning)—the two seats of national-socialist "philosophy"—and, beyond, from a bad (simultaneously weak and suspect) "romantic" overdetermination: that of Wagnerism, which in reality harbors, because it contains it in germ, everything that burdens national socialism and keeps it from being at the level of the task, or of the historial mission, that one might have thought it promised to achieve, misleading it into a technicist somnambulism and, by means of the racist ideology we know, the dream of an aesthetico-political organization (in what I have elsewhere thought it possible to call "national aestheticism").[10] Thus decoded, the message becomes this: the rupture with Wagner is not a minor or anecdotal incident; it translates Nietzsche's fundamental metaphysical position, under whose horizon the historial destiny of Europe and of the world is played out; and Germany, unbeknownst to itself, is in place to miss this destiny, which yet is essentially its destiny or of which it is, essentially, the depository.

If in this way the stakes are indissociably philosophical and political, exactly as is the case—Heidegger is the first to recognize it and to show why—in the Platonic regimentation of the question of art, this is so because in reality it is a matter of art in its relation to the political. The question has been, since Plato, that is to say, since Kant and the modern opening of the debate over Platonism: does art still—or can it still—give its essential direction and configuration to the being-in-community, city or people? Or concerning this role, which it will assume (because no philosophy issuing from the Kantian tradition has ever doubted this), is it not the case that, at one time or another, this role will necessarily be confided to philosophy itself, inasmuch as direction and configuration imply the revealing or the assignation of truth (and consequently of the good)? Or again, is it not the case that philosophy, against Kant if you will, that is to say remaining faithful to Plato, reaffirms itself in its most eminent possibility, and it is the end of art, at the very least, to speak like Hegel, in its "religious" vocation.

Or again, on the other hand, that the Kantian suspicion in regard to metaphysics grows more serious, and the question arises, not for a second time (because it has never arisen as such in the philosophical tradition) but for the first time, of the possibility of a "great art" that would have the force to supplement philosophy's political (or religious) loss of strength, which is the ineluctable consequence of a loss of strength as to the truth itself. This question, to different degrees, is that of the first romantics and Hölderlin, but it is also Nietzsche's question and Heidegger's. And it is visibly under its constraint that the sentence is pronounced, enigmatic from the first, about "the hostility of Nietzsche contra Wagner as the necessity of our History."

It remains to be seen, nevertheless, what Heidegger is aiming at under the name of Wagner. The artist, no doubt; that is to say, his art. But this art, what is it? Music? Theater? Musical drama as the restoration of tragedy? And behind the artist, is he thinking of the theoretician (of art and of his art), of ideology or politics, or even of the "phenomenon" that is already historical inasmuch as there exists, clearly, a "Wagnerism"? If it is a question of "great art," in other words, which forms the horizon of such a declaration, what part of this question applies to music? Would music be *essentially* responsible for Nietzsche's historial rupture with Wagner?

These questions become all the more necessary in that Heidegger's attention to music is, we know, nearly nil: beyond the discourse on Conradin Kreutzer (or for which Conradin Kreutzer is the pretext), "Memorial Address" (in *Discourse on Thinking*), which says practically nothing about music, allusions and references to music are extremely rare, and mostly conventional: for example, in *The Principle of Reason*, the application to Mozart, on the occasion of the 200th anniversary of his birth (and in the guise of the nth variation on the name of Amadeus?), of the distich of Angelus Silesius on the "lute of God."[11] And in that, above all, when he analyzes at length the Platonic treatment of the question of art in *The Republic* (in the first of his courses on Nietzsche: "The Will to Power as Art"), Heidegger moves quickly through Books II and III, of which he retains only the poetics and which he considers as simple preliminaries to Book X, and does not touch the question of music.

There is only one exception, at least to my knowledge, which is also not foreign to the enigmatic allusion, of historial import, that has concerned us until now: it is, in the same course on Nietzsche, and ultimately in a very expected manner, a fairly long argument consecrated to Wagner. Obviously one must consider it.

~

This argument is part of a section of the course entitled "Six Fundamental Facts Drawn from the History of Aesthetics." This section, to situate it briefly, was destined to show in what way the Nietzschean determination of art as figure and figuration (*Gestalt, Gestaltung*) of the Will to Power is inscribed in the properly aesthetic aim of the essence of art; and consequently to permit the comprehension of the rigorous meaning inebriation takes on, in Nietzsche's thought, as the fundamental aesthetic state. Taken in itself, this section is nothing else—even if Heidegger presents it as a simple observation—than a history of Occidental thought on art, sounded in its essential moments, that is to say, according to the successive "messages" on being that order History as such.

Heidegger thus calls "aesthetic," in the broader sense, the entirety of Occidental thinking on art. More precisely, the "aesthetic" in this sense, which is in fact very broad, coincides with the properly philosophical interpretation of art, that is to say with the interpretation inaugurated by Plato and Aristotle. Before that, says Heidegger, came what is to be understood as the time of Greek "great art" and of the "great philosophy" that preceded philosophy itself—and this prehistory constitutes, in a fairly strange way, the first period of this history in six periods—there is no room for anything like an "aesthetic":

> The magnificent art of Greece remains without a corresponding cog-
> nitive-conceptual meditation on it, such meditation not having to be

identical with aesthetics. The lack of such a simultaneous reflection or meditation on great art does not imply that Greek art was only "lived" [*erlebt*], that the Greeks wallowed in a murky brew of "experiences" [*Erlebnisse*] braced by neither concepts nor knowledge. It was their good fortune that the Greeks had no "lived experiences." On the contrary, they had such an original nature and luminous knowledge, such a passion for knowledge, that in their luminous state of knowing they had no need of "aesthetics."[12]

This *knowledge*, which renders any aesthetic useless and does not find in it anything like philosophy, is nothing else—Heidegger insists on it heavily at this time—than *tekhnè* in its original meaning, this meaning that tragic thinking, in particular Sophocles,[13] still keeps and that philosophy, precisely, begins by forgetting, as if ultimately, somehow, it were born of this very forgetting.

The aesthetic, then, only appears with philosophy in the strict sense (metaphysics), that is, "at the moment where the great art, but also the great philosophy that follows the same course, reaches its end." The aesthetic, that is to say, in general—this is the definition that Heidegger proposes—the *épistèmè* of the sensual and affective behavior of man and, in a more determined fashion, the "consideration of the affective state of man in his relation to the beautiful," is consequently overdetermined, all along its historic deployment, by the apparatus of "fundamental concepts" that were introduced by Plato and Aristotle "and that would delimit in the future the field of all interrogation on art."

That means, on the one hand, that if the term "aesthetic" is a recent formulation, "the thing itself that the name names with pertinence . . . is as old as the reflection on art and on the beautiful in occidental thought: . . . it is already as an aesthetic that philosophy begins to reflect on the essence of art and the beautiful." By means of which there is strictly no thinking on art and the beautiful, at least none that does not manage to remove itself from the philosophical, that could escape from the constraint of the aesthetic.

But that means, on the other hand, that the exclusive taking account of the affective state of man, *apropos* of art, necessarily pre-

supposes, even though obscurely at first, the scission between object and subject: the aesthetic will always envisage art from the
point of view of creation or reception (taste), never from that of
the work itself. Its *propos*, ultimately, will be not art (or the beautiful) but the relation of man—considered for the occasion as sen-
sibility, that is to say according to the metaphysical division itself—to art (or the beautiful).

In other words, Plato and Aristotle will have initially traced the
definitive closure of the aesthetic: no interrogation concerning art,
not even that of Hegel, who proclaims its end—but also, in this
historial area, no practice of art—will be able to enter it, or, it
comes to the same thing, will be able to free itself from the tutelage
of the fundamental concepts "struck" from the dawn of philosophy
(the very ones that Heidegger's lectures on "The Origin of the
Work of Art," roughly contemporary with the course, aim to de-
construct). Be it at least, against the background of Plato's eidetic
interpretation of being, not only the *hulè-morphè* (*materia-forma*)
couple as constitutive of *phainesthai* in general—of the self-show-
ing or appearing according to *eidos*, aspect or contour—but also
the assignation of the beautiful as *ekphanestaton* (shining or fullness
of appearing) and the "poietic" understanding of *tekhnè*, considered from then on, in the forgetfulness of its original meaning—
and on the model of artisanal fabrication—as a simple savoir faire.
At least, because it is evidently necessary to add to this list the
concept of *mimesis*, which is also presented five or six sections further on, without the shadow of any reserve, as the determining
concept for any understanding of art from the point of view of its
relation to the true. And because, in the same period, we see clearly
that Heidegger tries—with difficulty—to solicit (this is the Hegelian "result") a Platonic-Aristotelian prescription: the work of art
defined as the sensual presentation of a spiritual content, whence is
pronounced, in all rigor, that art is nevertheless a "thing past." The
first version of the lectures on the "Origin of the Work of Art"
(1935) says this, where everything is already brought together:

> All meditation on art and the artwork, all theory of art and aesthetics
> since the Greeks, has stood till the present hour beneath a *remark-*

able fate [*Verhängnis*]. The meditation on art began among the Greeks (Plato and Aristotle) with the characterization of the artwork as a fabricated thing, that is, as a tool-thing [*Zeugwerk*]. Accordingly, the artwork is viewed in the first place, and that means here in its actual being, as formed matter. At the same time, however, it could not remain concealed that, fundamentally, the artwork is indeed "more." Thus the view was held: the artwork—namely, the fabricated thing—says yet something other than what it is itself, *allo agoreuei* "allegory." The view was held: there is yet something else with which the artwork, that is, the fabricated thing, is brought together, *sumbollei* "symbol." . . .

Ever since, the distinctions between form and matter, content and meaning, shape and idea have provided the tools for grasping the artwork. And the fate [*Verhängnis*] consists precisely in the fact that these distinctions are always correct and can always be demonstrated; for the artwork always also admits to being considered as a fabricated thing which in addition presents a "spiritual meaning" [*geistigen Gehalt*]. Art is accordingly the representation [*Darstellung*] of something supra-sensual in a formed sensual matter.[14]

From this, it is clear, the task of a deconstruction of the aesthetic is sketched out. If this is the closure of the aesthetic, and its "fate," then, as Heidegger says, "Hegel's statement: 'But we no longer have an absolute need to bring a meaning to representation in the form of art'—remains true." At least, he adds, it does not become "a *question* . . . whether this truth is final. That is to say: whether the internal presuppositions of this statement, the traditional conception of the essence of art as representation, will always stand firm or whether they must be transformed in their very ground" (*Origin*, p. 54).

Such a "metamorphosis" of the understanding of the work of art constitutes the entire project of Heidegger in the years of "retreat"—when it was a question of enunciating, precisely, the truth of "national aestheticism." It certainly implies a philosophical decision: that of going further back than the concept of truth, which the eidetic interpretation of being necessitates or delimits, even to *alètheia* itself. And it is thus the concept of presentation, *Darstellung*, that we must attack, at the risk of (re)producing, after Aristotle, a new mixture of originary *mimesis* and of brutally affirming the *apophantic* character of *tekhnè*. Heidegger's meditation on art opens and is perhaps broken on this peremptory declaration: "The work of art, however, never represents anything [*stellt nie etwas dar*]; for the simple reason that it has nothing which it could represent, because the work creates [*schafft*] in the first place that which only through it enters into the open [*ins offene tritt*]."[15] But the "metamorphosis" *equally* implies a political decision inasmuch as the philosophical decision is immediately translated into terms of "spiritual decision" (*geistige Entscheidung*).[16] What is at play in the "metamorphosis," that is to say in the attempt "to surmount [*überwinden*] the aesthetic,"[17] is the historial destiny of Germany. For those who do not refuse to read it, the last lines of the lecture—like similar lines in the first commentary on Hölderlin—leave no incertitude. *Knowledge* as it relates to art—that is to say the response to the question: What is the work of art in its essence?—engages the "historial *Dasein*" of the Germans. Inasmuch as the response to the question of art, if it can be given, the sudden outbreak against the aesthetic "fatality" that has weighed on the Occident since the Greeks' betrayal of the "grandeur" of their own beginning, will be the only possible response to the question—which we must recognize as abyssal—that haunts Heideggerian predication at this time: Who are we? What about our *Dasein*, that is to say our *ek-sistence* in history as the capacity to open—or to reopen—History by virtue of an art that would be great again?

> This spiritual decision can only be *prepared through long labor*. It is not a question of the correctness or falseness of an aesthetic theory, rather what stands to decision is whether we know what art and the artwork can be and must be in our historical existence: an origin [*Ursprung*] and thus a leap forward [*Vorsprung*]—or rather something that is any longer just carried along and thus a mere addendum.
>
> This knowing or not knowing *in part* decides as to *who we are*. (*Origin*, p. 54)

~

It is against the background of this delimitation that the description of the four periods following the philosophical or metaphysical foundation of the aesthetic is articulated.

The first of them—the third, then, in this general history—is constituted by the entry of the aesthetic into the space of the metaphysics of Modern Times, that is to say into the space of the metaphysics of subjectivity: it is there that the aesthetic properly speaking is organized, the aesthetic in the narrow sense, which is essentially a theory of taste. Kant and Schiller however, we must note, are removed from this moment of the aesthetic to which they ordinarily seem to belong: the one for his determination of the beautiful as the object of a disinterested pleasure and of the behavior toward the beautiful as "free favor" (*freie Gunst*), the other for being the only one to have understood the essence of what the first one meant and to have drawn from it the consequences as to the "historial and foundational existence (*Dasein*) of the History of man"; both having also succumbed to the erroneous interpretations of the nineteenth century, starting with Schopenhauer's, of which Nietzsche remained the exemplary victim.[18]

The second of these periods, that is to say the fourth, witnessed the—Hegelian—accomplishment of the aesthetic, whose greatness, unequaled and probably unequalable, depends not only on its being the most vast, most powerful and comprehensive meditation on art that the Occident has ever willed us, even from the viewpoint of metaphysics, but also on this: that this aesthetic "recognized" and "pronounced" the "end of great art." A troubling motif: we believed art to be "finite" in its grandeur, that is to say in its capacity to "present the absolute" (in its "absolute power"), since the end of the fifth century in Athens; thus that a second death comes to it, contemporary with the deployment of the aesthetic *stricto sensu* and with the emergence of modern art, that is to say, ultimately, in romanticism. Heidegger's text, however, is clear:

> Concurrent with the formation of a dominant aesthetics and of the aesthetic relation to art in modern times is the decline of great art, great in the designated sense. Such decline does not result from the fact that the "quality" is poorer and the style less imposing; it is rather that art forfeits its essence, loses its immediate relation to the basic task of representing the absolute, i.e. of establishing the absolute definitively as such in the realm of historical man. . . .
>
> At the historical moment when aesthetics achieves its greatest pos-

sible height, breadth, and rigor of form, great art comes to an end. (*Nietzsche I*, p. 84)

Then comes the third period (the fifth), which is the Wagnerian period.

It is constituted, says Heidegger, precisely by the response that the nineteenth century "dares" to make to the fall or the decline of art, to its defection (*Abfall*) from its essence. It is thus the moment in which, against the Hegelian verdict, the nineteenth century "dares to undertake one more time the total work of art," the *Gesamtkunstwerk*.

This audacity and this effort are evidently "inseparable from the name of Wagner." But the entire century is concerned as well. However, this century—at least from the German point of view, the discourse of Heidegger is in this respect politically very clear— is "of the most equivocal": in its center, the decade of 1850–60, it offers the vision of a "confused and obscured" historial and spiritual situation. There "comes in . . . , on the one hand, the authentic and vivacious tradition of the great age of the German movement"—this is how Heidegger designates the last third of the eighteenth century, the great age, in effect, of the birth of German idealism, that is to say properly German philosophy—and, on the other hand, "the deaf and uprooting desolation of existence, which came to light during the years of the 'foundation of the Empire'" —which leads from the project of Bismarck to the "first third of the twentieth century." By which we must understand: up to 1930 (or 1933): it is a question not only of modern "uprooting," of Europe's entry into the devastating deployment of technology, but also, much more precisely, of Germany's decline, sanctioned by the defeat of 1918 and the unacceptable Treaty of Versailles.

From here, two fundamental questions arise:

1. Why is this Wagnerian period a determining period in the history of the aesthetic?

2. Why is the Wagnerian enterprise a "failure," and why is Nietzsche justified in having broken with Wagner?

Heidegger's whole argument is organized practically around these two questions.

~

The response to the first of these two questions is in reality double. First, the project of Wagner is fundamentally an aesthetic project, that is to say, a project that is only explained, as such, by the dominance of the aesthetic over art. One sign of this, but it is the surest, is that "it is accompanied and supported by a priori reflections and commentaries," that is to say by a theoretical preliminary (Heidegger recalls its principal characteristics) of such a nature that Wagner's "effort" "does not limit itself to the simple creation of works destined to such a goal: the *Gesamtkunstwerk.* Wagner's project is an aesthetic project because it is a *project*: the theorization of art and, even more, the auto-reflexivity of art are the "tribute," as Hegel said, that we must pay to the era, that is, to the undivided reign of Science from now on. From this point of view, Heidegger adheres without reserve to the Hegelian verdict: all will to "great art" is in advance marked by inanity because, following the Hegelian truth as the truth of the aesthetic itself, the birth of the aesthetic signifies the death of art, or, to say it less emphatically (but more rigorously), the very fact that there is an aesthetic implies the end—the passage or sublation—of art in its absolute destination. The Wagnerian enterprise is thus ultimately nothing but a simple aesthetic, even "aesthete," *restoration* of "great art," that is to say in the circumstances of tragedy. It is, literally, a decadent enterprise—if it is not simply, like any restoration, applied and laborious. And we must recognize here that the verdict is of an impeccable justice, whatever—manifest—abhorrence underlies it.

However, this enterprise, or rather, this "aspiration" to the total work of art—"although it must infallibly end up opposite to great art as much in its execution as in its effects"—remains unique in its era, and Wagner, "in spite of many propensities toward melodrama or adventure," by far outdoes other contemporary "efforts" "in his concern to safeguard the essentialness of art in existence." In other terms: the Wagnerian enterprise is perhaps aesthetic or aestheticizing, yet it is unique, and it represents, after the Hegelian accomplishment of the aesthetic, the final outbreak, coming from the aesthetic, against the presupposition of the aesthetic itself, that

is to say against the recognition and acceptance—more or less clear
up to Hegel—of the end of "great art." There, it is certain, Wagner
only verifies the law according to which all art, under the surveil-
lance of the aesthetic, is nostalgic for the "great art" that he undertakes—in vain—to restore. But from there, at the same time,
he takes the aesthetic to its limit, that is to say to the brink of its
destruction (at least in the sense that Nietzsche will attempt to
"radicalize" Wagner, at the cost, it is true, of a rupture that was
also "radical"). Wagner's enterprise is in some way the photographic negative of the Hegelian accomplishment of the aesthetic.
And first in that it not only aims to bring to an end the deadly separation of the arts (from this point of view, too, the *Gesamtkunstwerk* is only the product, or rather the result, of a fairly elementary
"summation") but also aims, and such is its "concern to safeguard
the essentialness of art in existence," to "constitute a celebration of
the community of the people [*Volksgemeinschaft*]—we know to
what extent the word, at that time, was charged with a terrible political connotation—thus presenting itself as "*the* religion itself":
"*die*" *Religion.* The ultimate audacity of the aesthetic, its ultimate
action, is thus the ultimately romantic desire (even if Heidegger, as
almost always, wants to know nothing about this)[19] for a *religious,*
that is to say *political,* art, in the sense that Attic tragedy, according
to his idealist myth, is such a "solemnity" (*Feier*), the festival and
celebration of the people or of the City. What would in sum save
Wagner from the aesthetic—or from aestheticism—would be the
recognition and affirmation of the historial destiny of art.

Why, then, is this enterprise a failure?

Here is Heidegger's explanation—he has just defined the *Gesamtkunstwerk*:

> In that respect the definitive arts are musical and literary [*Dichtung*].
> Theoretically, music is to be a means for achieving effective drama; in
> reality, however, music in the form of opera becomes the authentic
> art. Drama possesses its importance and essential character not in po-
> etic originality, that is, not in the well-wrought truth of the linguistic
> work [*in der dichterischen Ursprünglichkeit, d.h. der gestalteten Wahr-
> heit des Sprachwerkes*], but in things pertaining to the stage, theatrical

arrangements and gala productions. Architecture serves merely for theater construction, painting provides the backdrops, sculpture portrays the gestures of actors. Literary creation and language remain without the essential and decisive shaping force of genuine knowledge. What is wanted is the domination of art as music, and thereby the domination of the pure state of feeling. (*Nietzsche 1*, p. 86)

On the condition that we understand clearly and do not fear shortcuts, that can only mean one single thing: Wagner, despite his obscure intuition of the historial destination of art (but also for want of a sufficiently clear attitude vis-à-vis the innumerable programs in his century of aesthetic politics), is the opposite of Hölderlin, the only one in Heidegger's eyes whose *knowledge* concerning art and History measures up to the destiny, such as it was then in operation, of Germany and the Occident. Several pages later, Heidegger opposes Hölderlin to Nietzsche himself, crediting him with a more "profound" and "noble" interpretation of the antagonism between the Dionysian and the Apollonian. And its admonition is perfectly clear:

It is enough if we gather from the reference that the variously named conflict of the Dionysian and the Apollonian, of holy passion and sober representation, is a hidden stylistic law of the historical determination of the German people, and that one day we must find ourselves ready and be able to give it shape [*Gestaltung*]. The opposition is not a formula with the help of which we should be content to describe "culture." By recognizing this antagonism Hölderlin and Nietzsche early on placed a question mark after the task of the German people to find their essence historically. Will we understand this cipher? One thing is certain: history will wreak vengeance on us if we do not.[20]

It is precisely this kind of cipher that Wagner's work does not include. First, because language as such remains subordinate in it, and consequently the work lacks the *Dichtung*, in its original meaning and function. However, with the *Dichtung*, it is not only "science properly speaking" that loses strength, that is to say *tekhnè*, in the Hölderlinian or Sophoclean sense. It is also the very

power of such a science, the "figural force": *die gestalterische Kraft.*
No figure, no *Gestalt,* in truth, can arise or detach itself from an art
that refuses even in its principles the very element of figuration, of
Gestaltung: language or speech, *die Sprache,* which is in its essence
secret, as the contemporary lectures on "The Origin of the Work
of Art" recall, *die Sage*—that is to say, in its fullest sense, *mythos.*[21]
Wagner's art is incapable of "myth," of "essential and decisive"
speech, which alone would be equal to producing or establishing
the figure in which the "historial destination of the Germans"
could be recognized. That is why this art, despite its ambition, is
not one, or at least is not "great." Not only are Wagner's "operatic
poems" weak or complacent—and forced—in the Germanic or
Nordic "remythologizing" (Greece is missing here, which is the
only yardstick for Germany), but the primacy of music, in this
art, is the most evident sign of its failure inasmuch as, translating
the "reign of the pure affective state," it presupposes a purely aesthetic apprehension of art. Heidegger defines it in the following
manner:

> That Richard Wagner's attempt had to fail does not result merely
> from the predominance of music with respect to the other arts in his
> work. Rather, that the music could assume such preeminence at all
> has its grounds in the increasingly aesthetic posture taken toward art
> as a whole—it is the conception and estimation of art in terms of the
> unalloyed state of feeling and the growing barbarization of the affec-
> tive state to the point where it becomes the sheer bubbling and boil-
> ing of feeling abandoned to itself. (*Nietzsche 1,* pp. 87–88)

Here we must stop for a moment: not only were these words
("barbarization of the affective state") pronounced in 1936, at the
very moment when the Wagnerian ceremony served as a standard
for the Nazi aestheticization of politics, but under such a determination of the aesthetic, something fundamental about the essence
of music, and thus about the essence of art, was being played out.
    We will note first of all that, in this diagnosis or verdict, Hei-
degger subscribes without reserve to the Nietzschean condemnation of Wagner. When he spoke of the "reign of the pure affective

state," Heidegger, who did not miss this occasion to attack one more time the ideology of the "lived experience," thus made explicit the "state" in question:

> . . . the tumult and delirium of the senses, tremendous contraction, the felicitous distress that swoons in enjoyment, absorption in "the bottomless sea of harmonies," the plunge into frenzy and the disintegration into sheer feeling as redemptive. The "lived experience" as such becomes decisive. The work is merely what arouses such experience. All portrayal is to work its effects as foreground and superficies, aiming toward the impression, the effect, wanting to work on and arouse the audience: theatrics. Theater and orchestra determine art. (ibid., p. 86)

What he incriminated in this manner was obviously the dubious erotics, simultaneously sentimental and voluptuous, effusive and "mystical," that are the clearest content of the "affective state." But in the same movement, it is also its "theatricalization" that reinforces the music in diluting the stage itself, thus forbidding all presentation, all real *Darstellung*, ruining in advance any possibility of the appearance of an authentic *Gestalt*. Moreover, Heidegger then cited a passage of Wagner's *Work of Art of the Future*, which in fact says: "the orchestra dissolves in some way the inert, inanimate floorboards of the real stage, in a fluid expanse, without resistance, receptive, impressionable, ethereal, and of which the immeasurable depth is the sea of sentiment itself." And to this he opposes "what Nietzsche says about Wagner's means of obtaining his effect," citing number 839 of the old *Will to Power*:

> Consider the means of achieving effects to which Wagner most likes to turn (and which for the most part he had to invent): to an astonishing extent they resemble the means by which the hypnotist achieves his effect (his selection of tempi and tonal hues for his orchestra; a repulsive avoidance of the logic and intervals of rhythm; the lingering, soothing, mysterious, hysterical quality of his "endless melody"). And is the state to which the prelude to *Lohengrin* reduces its listeners, especially the lady listeners, essentially different from that of a somnambulistic trance?—I heard an Italian woman who had just listened

to that prelude say, flashing those lovely mesmerized eyes that Wag-
neriennes know how to affect, "How one falls *asleep* with this music!" (*Nietzsche 1*, pp. 86–87)

Heidegger not only subscribes to this Nietzschean condemnation but also justifies Nietzsche's rupture with Wagner by the same
motif. As we might expect, it is a matter of the *Gestaltung*, that is
to say, of the question of knowing "if art is still known and willed
as the normative figuration and preservation [*als massgebende
Gestaltung und Bewahrung*] of beings as a whole" (ibid., p. 89):

> And yet such arousal of frenzied feeling and unchaining of "affects"
> could be taken as a rescue of "life," especially in view of the growing
> impoverishment and deterioration of existence occasioned by indus-
> try, technology, and finance, in connection with the enervation and
> depletion of the constructive forces [*bildende Kraft*] of knowledge and
> tradition, to say nothing of the lack of every establishment of goals for
> human existence. Rising on swells of feeling would have to substitute
> for a solidly grounded and articulated position [*eine gegründete und
> gefügte Stellung*] in the midst of being, the kind of thing that only
> great poetry and thought can create [*das grosse Dichten und Denken*].
>   It was the frenzied plunge into the whole of things in Richard
> Wagner's person and work that captivated the young Nietzsche; yet
> his captivation was possible only because something correlative came
> from him, what he then called the Dionysian. But since Wagner
> sought sheer upsurgence of the Dionysian upon which one might
> ride, while Nietzsche sought to leash its force and give it form [*seine
> Bändigung und Gestaltung*], the breach between the two was already
> predetermined. (ibid., p. 88)

Thus there was, in the Apollonian—that is to say, in what Hölderlin, more profoundly, would have ascribed to "Occidental sobriety"—something to resist the dubious, and finally decadent,
charm of the aestheticizing dissolution to which the emphatic
velleities of a "great art" led. And the rupture attests to this: Nietzsche was this resistance—which we could call "figural"—to
Dionysiac complacency and to affective abandon. The resistance of
"great art." Not that he had himself, or in his work, gotten involved in the path of "great art": Heidegger will always deny him

the right to such a pretension and will himself obstinately refuse to consider *Zarathustra*, for example, as a work of *Dichtung*.[22] But his rigorous dualism will have permitted him to reveal Wagnerian artifice and the dubious or watered-down nature of "restorations." This is after all why, outside of the "slipping into a falsely moralizing Christianity, mixed with ardor, concupiscence, and swooning," the essential complaint that Heidegger retains from Nietzsche is the absence of *style* in Wagner, which corresponds to the weakness of internal feeling, even the "scorn" in which Wagner holds internal feeling: "This is what Nietzsche expressed in the following manner: with Wagner 'one is floating and swimming,' instead of 'walking and dancing'—(meaning a blur instead of measure and step)." And we see clearly what he turns away from: the absence of style, in Wagner, is the inability to *figure*. And the inability to *figure* is the lack of *rhythm* (walk, step: cadence). The entire question is there. Because rhythm is not simply about cadence. And because cadence (walk or step) is about man: *Mann* or *vir*—and not *Mensch* or *homo*. The humanity of man, in his historial *Dasein*, presupposes an essential virility: a properly heroic capacity.

~

What Heidegger fundamentally subscribes to, de facto, is this: that an art founded on music (on the orchestra), that is to say, an art founded on the aesthetic apprehension of art and, in the last resort, conceived and organized from the viewpoint of an exclusive regard for affect, is an art that aims only for effect or impression (recurrent terms throughout these pages, as they are in Nietzsche's texts), and that is based only on its reception, or implies in its principle only a call to a pure passivity. According to a very old, very profound, and very solid equivalence—perhaps indestructible—it is a *feminine* art, destined for women or for the feminine part of men. It is a *hysterical* art, in every sense. And for this reason, essentially, music *is* hysteria. At least, a particular music.

An explanation is necessary here.

We will have noticed that the clinical picture, in the Nietzschean diagnostic, is rigorous and complete: Nietzsche speaks of Wagnerian music in terms of the hypnosis and somnambulistic ecstasy in the effects it produces. He even describes the hysteria—of unending melody. In another metaphorical register, but one that is nonetheless clinical and that has more than a single relation to the question of hysteria and hypnosis, Nietzsche speaks equally often of Wagnerian music in terms of a drug, opium, an anesthetic. And when Heidegger takes up Nietzsche's remark in a more "metaphysical" register—and not missing an opportunity, either, to incriminate the "fatal" influence of the "metaphysics" of Schopenhauer—he is not saying anything different: "the dissolution of everything solid into a fluid, flexible, malleable state, into a swimming and floundering; the unmeasured, without laws or borders, clarity or definiteness; the boundless night of sheer submergence" (*Nietzsche 1*, p. 87). It would be pointless, I imagine, to underline the allusions to *Tristan*, which would be on this issue, to borrow a formula from Nietzsche himself, the *opus hystericum* par excellence, that is to say, the *opus estheticum* par excellence.[23] Here hysteria, or the aesthetic state, is to be understood as the height of passivity, that is to say as the height of plasticity, malleability, impressionability. As pure "materiality," if we prefer, according to—again—a very old equivalence (*materia/mater*), which, beyond any particular etymological resource of any particular natural language, is also anchored in the Aristotelian—if not more ancient—determination of femininity or the essence of the feminine.[24]

To this passivity is opposed the virile gesture of "great art": *style* as Nietzsche in fact says—and the word, as Jacques Derrida has shown, is not without sexual connotation.[25] Or what Heidegger calls the *Gestaltung*: figuration or configuration, putting into form, or "structuration" as Klossowski usually translates it—but there is no satisfactory translation, not even "fiction" or "fiction-ing," that I have found other than the Latin *fingere*. *Gestaltung* is the violent imposition of form (Heidegger, faithful to Nietzsche's Apollonianism, imagines it as the sculptor's gesture, that is to say, as the *plastic* gesture par excellence, the one Nietzsche reclaims when he speaks of philosophizing "with a hammer"). It is the marking, the *Prägung*—the seal or sealing that makes appear, in some malleable matter or other (wax, for example) the *sigillum*, the effigy. To designate an operation of this kind, the Greeks used the verb *tupein*, from *tupos*: the blow, the mark, the imprint, the engraved characters, even the sculpture or the image in relief. We have *typer* in French; we should be able to say *typization*, typing. But on the condition of thinking that what thus takes form or figure also stands or is erected, installed in the literal sense, or made a *stele*— if, as I have tried to show elsewhere, we have no other equivalents in our language to render the meaning or meanings that in German are clustered around the radical *stellen* (*Gestalt, Darstellung, Herstellung, Vorstellung,* etc.), which Heidegger continually plays on in his determination of the essence of the work of art as *Gestell*.[26]

Gestaltung is properly virile; Heidegger insists on this a great deal: citing Nietzsche himself ("Our aesthetics heretofore has been a woman's aesthetics, inasmuch as only the recipients of art have formulated their experiences of 'what is beautiful.' In all philosophy to date the artist is missing," *Nietzsche 1*, p. 70), he demonstrates clearly that the greatness of Nietzsche's project is the desire to transform or convert the aesthetic from the feminine that it was into a masculine or virile aesthetic, that is to say, an aesthetic guided by the point of view of the artist or creator. Whence Nietzsche "pushes the aesthetic to the extreme," just to the point where—as with Kant, although in a less radical way—it "turns against itself" and, if it does not destroy itself as such (Nietzsche did not take this step), indicates at least, from the interior of the aesthetic, the place where such a destruction presents itself as necessary. It is also what saves Nietzsche and delivers him to the "task of questioning," he who otherwise remains penned in by the metaphysics of the Will to Power and, as a consequence, by the aesthetic taken to its limit as a "physiology of art." And who is thus submitted, as the final moment of this history of the aesthetic shows with precision, to the nihilism that, contrary to Hegel, that is to say without the Hegelian clairvoyance, he puts into question not in art itself but in morality, religion, and philosophy. In spite of himself, and in spite of his rupture with Wagner.

Thus it is *Gestaltung* versus hysteria. Or *Gestaltung* versus nihilism. On the question of Wagner himself, the thing is perfectly clear, even if only because the great leader of this so-called nihilism is in reality Schopenhauer. When he speaks, with the most obvious scorn, of the "unmeasured, without laws or borders, clarity or definiteness; the boundless night of sheer submergence . . . ," Heidegger adds:

> In other words, art is once again to become an absolute need. But now the absolute is experienced as sheer indeterminacy, total dissolution into sheer feeling, a hovering that gradually sinks into nothingness. No wonder Wagner found the metaphysical confirmation and explanation of his art in Schopenhauer's main work, which he studied diligently four different times. (ibid., p. 87)

On the other hand, on the question of Nietzsche, nothing is so clear-cut. Because the *Gestaltung*, in the years of the "explication" with Nietzsche—the "political" years—is still, for Heidegger, on the program. The delimitation of Nietzsche, it must not be forgotten, means also a "rescue," a sort of *Rettung*, as Benjamin would have said. Not of the "philosophy of Nietzsche" as such, even though it is a matter of demonstrating that it exists and of affirming its greatness, but of an "inspiration" that the contemporary teaching on Hölderlin proves it is not vain to qualify as "heroic." That is why Heidegger can retain from Nietzsche—and from a certain Nietzschean posterity represented, for example, by Jünger—more or less without reserve, a veritable obsession with the *Gestaltung*. The declaration of the principle that opens the recapitulation of the history of the aesthetic is completely explicit in this regard:

> For, in truth, the fact of whether and how an era is committed to an aesthetic, whether and how it adopts a stance toward art of an aesthetic character, is decisive for the way art shapes the history [*geschichtebildend*] of that era—or remains irrelevant for it.
> Because what stands in question for us is art as a configuration [*Gestalt*] of will to power, which is to say, as a configuration of Being in general, indeed the distinctive one, the question of aesthetics as the basic sort of meditation on art and the knowledge of it can be treated

only with respect to fundamentals. Only with the help of a reflection on the essence of aesthetics developed in this way can we get to the point where we can grasp Nietzsche's interpretation of the essence of art; only with the help of such a reflection can we at the same time take a position with regard to Nietzsche's interpretation, so that on this basis a *differential explication* [*Auseinandersetzung*] can flourish.[27]

The "differential explication," we know, will bear on the Will to Power or, if one prefers, on Nietzsche's ontology. But not on the *Gestalt*. And this is ultimately what explains that, if Heidegger really *critiques* Nietzsche, he does not critique the Nietzschean critique of Wagner. The hostility to Catholicism, and consequently to Wagner's "pious" leanings, certainly enters into this indulgence. But not this alone: we must remember the "defect of style"—surely the major complaint. An absence of rhythm, Heidegger called it. But it was still a matter of "figure" or of "type," if it is true, as Heidegger himself recalled,[28] that *rhuthmos*, originally, signifies *das Gepräge*, the mark or the imprint.

～

It is thus an onto-typology[29] that organizes the deconstruction of the aesthetic and forges Heidegger's complicity with Nietzsche contra Wagner—in all its political consequences. However, the "reign of art as music," the primacy of affect and impression, passivity and hysteria, are not the only issues. Or rather, if they are at issue, it is because they do not after all produce anything but a theater or, as Heidegger called it with even greater scorn, "some theater" ("*Theater*").

The close relationship between hysteria and theatricality in all discourse on hysteria (from Plato to Lacan) is well known. Hysteria has always been imagined as *commedia*, dramatization, false semblance, ostentatious play. And imagined as such because it is fundamentally mimetic. As soon as there is theater, there is *mimesis*, and first of all in the sense of imitation through identification. A passive *mimesis*, then: that of the spectator or auditor. For example, says Plato—but this is more than *an* example, it is *the* very example of all examples, the *exemplum* of *exempla*—the mimesis of the children who listen to the stories, pernicious in every way, of which myths are made, and who are marked by them in an indelible way, no longer able to live, for the rest of their lives, except in imitation. But also in the sense of this sort of *mimesis*, apparently more active and virile (in any case, this is what Diderot thinks), that is properly the actor's *mimesis*, he who plays a role, and that is, in Plato's eyes at least, just as pernicious and dangerous (and thus, if we wish, "feminine" or without possible conversion to virility) in that it presupposes in principle, as the examination of modes of poetic enunciation (dramatic, epic, dithyrambic) attests to, a fundamental disappropriation—he who acts onstage does not act for himself and does not speak in his proper name—a disappropriation responsible for the spectator's identification, itself disappropriating, because it is only a game. *Mimesis* is always a matter of disappropriation.

I cannot here go over analyses that I have developed at length elsewhere. I would simply like to recall this: in the detailed commentary on *The Republic* that he is next led to produce from the point of view of the problematic of art and of *mimesis* (in view of understanding how, in Nietzsche, the "reversal of Platonism" merges with the recognition of a terrifying "discord between art and truth"), if Heidegger pays strictly no attention to this first and fundamental definition of *mimesis*, it is because he ultimately shares Plato's prejudice in regard to *mimesis* and theater. Moreover, he will manifest it on more than one occasion.[30] The same apropos of Nietzsche: not for one moment does Heidegger take up the texts, which he nevertheless cites, that deal with what Nietzsche calls "the problem of the actor," and in which, as well, one sees Nietzsche in turn share the Platonic prejudice. Such, for example, is the premise—the final one—of a project of general aesthetics entitled "On the Physiology of Art":

> 17. Problem of the *actor*. The "dishonesty," the typical ability to meta-
> · morphose as a *flaw in character*. . . . The Hanswurst, the clown, the
> buffo, the Gil Blas, the actor who plays the artist . . . (Cited in *Nietz-
> sche I*, p. 94)

Does such an underground residue of Platonism—and thus, in a pure paradox, of the aesthetic itself (in the broadest sense)—explain Nietzsche's and Heidegger's hostility, if not to music, at least to a particular music?

We know that Plato does not condemn all music, any more than he condemns all poetry, but that as a pure and simple consequence of the discrimination exercised apropos of *muthopoiesis*, under the double face of *logos* and *lexis*, of enunciations and the mode of enunciation (in the City, only poets telling the truth about the divine, and in a simple mode, will be tolerated: *haplè dièg̀esis*), he accepts in music only that which encourages virile and warlike behaviors (let us not forget that it is a question of the education of the "guardians" here). It is thus on the principle of the difference between activity and passivity, virility and femininity, that the division between the good harmonic modes (Dorian and Phyrigian) and the bad (Lydian) is constructed; the good instruments (instruments with simple stringing) and the bad (instruments with numerous strings, percussion, and most of all, the *aulos*), the good rhythms (simple, here again) and the bad (complex). However, this whole analysis depends solely upon the certitude that "rhythm and harmony are particularly suited to penetrate into the soul and to touch it forcefully" (*Republic*, 401d)—which, pending further evidence, seems very much to be the first and last word on music in Western philosophy.

It is the same principle, and the same certitude, that governs Nietzsche's rupture with Wagner: Wagner is enervation, sleepiness and torpor, submission, being-penetrated. Rossini or Bizet are lightness, energy, the intensification of life, joy and the pride of standing-up-straight, "striding and dancing" (cited in *Nietzsche 1*, p. 88). But it is also the principle, and up to a certain point the certitude, that supports Heidegger's approbation of the Nietzschean condemnation, and that even accentuates it because in appearance nothing in music escapes the aesthetic, that is to say the "reign of affect." Not even rhythm, we are to believe, except when it reveals the promise of a figural force. Assuredly Heidegger is too aware, he knows too well whence proceeds the Nietzschean perspective of a reversal of a "feminine" aesthetic into a "virile" aesthetic. And when he says, "Nietzsche's aesthetic inquiry explodes its own posi-

tion when it advances to its own most far-flung border," it is simultaneously a recognition that, from there, "aesthetics is by no
means overcome [*überwunden*]," adding, which is also perfectly
clear: "such overcoming requires a still more original metamorphosis of our *Dasein* and knowledge, which is something that
Nietzsche only *indirectly* prepares by means of the whole of his
metaphysical thought" (*Nietzsche 1*, p. 131). Nevertheless: the
"struggle" that Nietzsche led "to render possible the art of the
grand style"—if such is really the last word of his thinking on
art—still leads the way.

That is why it is necessary to tear the style-affirming Nietzsche
from his era, that is to say from the aesthetic and from everything
it can authorize. The political position taken is unequivocal:

> However often and however fatal [*fatal*] the way in which Nietzsche,
> both in language and in thought, was diverted into purely physiolog-
> ical, naturalistic assertions about art, it is an equally fatal misunder-
> standing on our part when we isolate such physiological thoughts and
> bandy them about as a "biologistic" aesthetics. It is even worse to
> confuse them with Wagner. We turn everything inside out when we
> make a philosophy of orgiastics out of it, as Klages does, thoroughly
> falsifying matters by proclaiming it Nietzsche's authentic teaching and
> genuine accomplishment.
>
> *In order to draw near to the essential will of Nietzsche's thinking, and*
> *remain close to it, our thinking must acquire enormous range, plus the*
> *ability to see beyond everything that is fatally contemporary in Nietzsche.*
> (*Nietzsche 1*, p. 127)

However, under this condition, in which the hostility to Wagner is
confirmed, the "reversal" (the *Umkehrung*) of, for example, the
Schopenhauerian definition of art as a "life calmer" into a definition of art as a "life stimulator" is not at all in the figure of the re-
newal of the same: "The reversal is the transformation of the determination of art into its essence." The height of the view is also
valid for a *decision* that History requires be made in regard to
Nietzsche's thinking:

> Such thinking about art is philosophical thought, setting the stan-
> dards through which historial explication [*geschichtliche Auseinander-*

setzung] comes to be, prefiguring [*Vorgestaltung*] what is to come. This is something to consider, if we wish to decide in what sense Nietzsche's question concerning art can still be aesthetics, and to what extent it in any case must be such. (ibid., p. 130)

And this decision—contra Wagner, one last time—is nothing other than the very affirmation of *style*, because in style, that is to say in the possibility of figuration, is put into play what governs all History: the law (*das Gesetz*), a word we must understand, in all probability, not in its Kantian sense but in the sense that the interpretation and the "situation" of Hölderlin allow, if the commentator gives himself the "right" to consider art as the presentation of the law:[31]

What Nietzsche says . . . with respect to music and in regard to Wagner applies to art as a whole:

"We no longer know how to *ground* the concepts 'model,' 'master,' 'perfection'—in the realm of values we grope blindly with the instincts of old love and admiration; we nearly believe that 'what is good is what pleases *us*. . . .'"

In opposition to the "complete dissolution of style" in Wagner, rules and standards, and above all the grounding of such, are here demanded clearly and unequivocally. . . .

Art is not only subject to rules, must not only obey laws, but is in itself legislation. Only as legislation is it truly art. What is inexhaustible, what is to be created, is the law [*Das Unerschöpfliche und zu Schaffende ist das Gesetz*]. Art that dissolves style in sheer ebullition of feelings misses the mark, in that its discovery of law is essentially disturbed; such discovery can become actual in art only when the law drapes itself in the freedom of a form [*Gestalt*] in order in that way to come openly into play.[32]

As a consequence we must understand, what is all the same barely encouraging, that the figure, the *Gestalt*, is the presentation—of course *without presentation*—of the law. The law is authorized only by art, or, it comes to the same thing, it is art alone that founds the law. Art is in the political principle as such; this cannot be more clearly said. Yet it is apparent that the fundamental mimetology that subtends Heidegger's conception of art comes to be condensed within the concept of law: the law is nothing other than the *articulation* (a derivative of *ars*, as we know) of the relation between *phusis* (the "inextinguishable" here, or what the lectures on the "Origin of the Work of Art" call the "Earth") and *tekhnè* (the "creatable" or the "to-be-created"; in the lectures, the "World"). It is in the very site of *polémos*, which the authority of Heraclitus doubtless does not forbid translating as *Kampf*, even when *Streit* would have been euphemistically preferable.[33] Such a law is historiality itself, the opening of History in its possibility. And because as such—that is to say as *origin* of History, or the political—it could not be presented, it returns to the figure to indicate it. Or to incarnate it. Art must present the unpresentability of what it proceeds from: that is to say the combat, which it *is*, against nature. And the figure is only the figure—absolutely sublime, we must believe[34]—of this combat. The figure of the political.

Heideggerian mimetology is very deeply political. It thinks itself to be, and offers itself as, the truth, until then dissimulated—even to the eyes of Nietzsche, who nonetheless presented it—of this weak mimetology inherited from Platonism and from the modern aesthetic that only ever authorizes a politics of affective effusion, or a political aestheticism. But was it sufficient to demarcate itself, in this mode, from mimetic passivity—and from political aestheticism—to really produce a *political* distinction?

Obviously the question would not arise if the call to the *decision* were not *also* made in solidarity, or complicity, with the well-known politics. That is to say with what I thought justified in calling "national aestheticism."

The deconstruction of the aesthetic was a necessary task—in the best of cases it is a matter, for art, of a liberation from philosophical tutelage—and probably an inevitable task—inasmuch as philosophy was condemned to be liberated, or to be delivered, from itself. This task, we see, remained unfinished: it was interrupted, as if wrecked somehow on the rock of politics. Thus it falls to us to accomplish it, or at least to pursue it. And we guess where that necessarily leads us: to the place where we have obstinately tried to *articulate* art and the political together, and to bring them into league with one another. As a concept of this *re-ligion*, the figure remains to be destroyed.

~

(One last word: given the radicality of the deconstruction, is the fate that Heidegger thus reserves for music the sign that no discourse on music other than the Platonic one [the aesthetic] can hold, or that no approach other than mimetology can be offered to us if we seek to imagine the essence of musical effect? Is it the sign, in other words, that music is unthinkable outside of *affection*?

The fact that, since Wagner, in the measure to which nihilism is deployed, music, with even more powerful means than those Wagner himself was given, has not ceased to invade our world and manifestly to take the lead over all other forms of art—including the arts of the image—the fact that "musicolatry" has relayed idolatry, is perhaps the first part of a response. Perhaps. But then we are far from being delivered from the aesthetic. And we are scarcely more advanced when it comes to what we must understand by [and do with] affect.)

§4 Adorno

> Prose isolates itself so ascetically from poetry for the sake of invoking song.
>
> Just as, according to Benjamin, painting and sculpture translate the mute language of things into a higher but similar one, so it might be supposed that music rescues name as pure sound—but at the cost of severing it from things.
>
> Perhaps the strict and pure concept of art is applicable only to music, while great poetry or great painting—precisely the greatest—necessarily brings with it an element of subject-matter transcending aesthetic confines, undissolved in the autonomy of form.
>
> —Adorno

It is no doubt not impossible to say that ultimately Wagner *saturated* opera. One proof of this, albeit an indirect one, is that everything that followed, without being exempt from the tremendous ambition he had imposed, bears the stigmata of an ending. It may be found in the nostalgic and relatively comfortable mode that the late Strauss resigned himself to, who ended his career summarily with an "adieu," more disenchanted than deeply melancholic, to the two genres in which, he must have surely recognized, a limit had been reached (this is why the so-called *Four Last Lieder*, if only because they return to a "law of genre," that is to say, to a pre-Mahlerian form of the *Lied*, have a meaning analogous to that of the self-reflection "in the manner of" that orders *Capriccio*). But it may also be found in the mode of redundancy, and thus of oversaturation, for which the early Strauss was renowned (or the Schönberg of the *Gurrelieder*), and in the pathos with which the Puccini of *Turandot* exhausted himself. Or again it may be found in the more equivocal and more subtle (more "French") mode of destructuration à la Debussy. Or, finally, in the style of properly modern radicality, the style of violent rupture and of incompleteness, "failure": Berg's *Lulu*, Schönberg's *Moses and Aaron*. And here, incontestably, things are far more serious. One might say—not only because it ups the ante where the means of expression are concerned (a move that Nietzsche had already denounced as an art subordinated to seeking an effect), but rather because of its *systematic* character, in the strict sense of the term—that Wagner's work left to his posterity a task every bit as impossible as the one left in philosophy by German idealism (Hegel) to its great successors: to continue to pursue what is completed. Thus, just as we have been able to describe the "Hegelian closure" of philosophy, we could describe a Wagnerian closure of opera. And even of art itself, or great art, as it was called at the time, because this was its "ambition." As a result of their anti-Hegelianism, what Wagner's writings and Nietzsche's *The Birth of Tragedy* most clearly demonstrate is that in wishing to overcome (*überwinden*) opera and all its "culture,"[1] Wagner devotes himself, with the *Gesamtkunstwerk*, to a totalizing sublation, to an *Aufhebung*, of all the arts, and to a *restoration* of "great art," more powerful because more modern (in fact, via other technical means): a restoration, of course, of Greek tragedy. At the same time, if the other arts were able to move in another direction—and were guided from the outset by another concept of "great" and another intuition of "art"—opera, itself a recent art though it might claim to be ancient, underwent such a severe declaration of completion. In fact, it was not sublated there, or was scarcely so.

To saturate here means simply: too much music; or if we prefer, despite the paradox, too much "Italianism," and too much credit given to the *Prima la musica*. In short it is the belief in music's "sublational" capacity (or, as he would say, its "synthesizing" capacity) that destroys for Wagner any chance of acceding to "totality" and, condemning him to choose sides in what is after all just the classical dilemma of opera, forces him into musical saturation. Saturation is a false totalization, at least insofar as it testifies to the false character of any will to totalization, even a "conceptual" one. On this point at least, although for entirely different reasons, Heidegger and Adorno agree with each another, and both of them attribute the responsibility for this unrestrained, "infinite" melocentrism to Schopenhauer, to the metaphysics of "feeling" and the "unconscious" (to the vague mysticism, Adorno says, of "thalassic regression"). Wagner definitively addressed only the problem of opera, to the nearly exclusive benefit of music, and not that of theater, where, considering the theater *à l'italienne,* his innovations are rather scanty. Or to put it otherwise, as a *Dichterkomponist* (a monstrous term, as Adorno remarks) Wagner confused language with "words" and music with the essence of language, its origin and its assumption. In the demonstration he conducts in the "Music Drama" chapter of *In Search of Wagner,* Adorno cites some passages that are in a sense damning:

> Science has laid bare to us the organism of language, but what she showed us was a dead organism, which only the poet's utmost can bring to life again, namely, by suturing the wounds with which the anatomist's scalpel has gashed the body of language and by breathing into it the breath that may animate it with living motion. This breath, however, is—music. . . .
>
> The necessary bestowal from within oneself, the seed that can only in the most ardent transports of love condense itself from its noblest forces—which grows only in order to be released, that is, to be released for the purposes of fertilization, indeed which is in and of itself [*an sich*] this more or less materialized drive—this procreative seed is the poetic intention, which brings to the gloriously loving woman, Music, the stuff for bearing.[2]

Despite their erotico-dialectical pathos (the same pathos, though less rigorous, or as Adorno would say more "voluptuous," than that which governs the opening paragraphs of *The Birth of Tragedy*), texts of this genre have at least one merit: they reveal the reason why all operas that have seriously tried to resist Wagnerian saturation, leaving aside those that have deliberately renounced totalization (this is above all true of Berg), have taken the form of a sort of "performative" meditation on the essence of language (of speech) in its relation to music. And thus on the very nature of the opera form. In Strauss, who is the most belated and no doubt the most "informed," the protocol, under its slightly belabored eighteenth-century elegance, is relatively coarse, even if it manifests a certain understanding of what is at stake. But really, to take as a subject the Quarrel of the Buffos or that of the Puccinists and the Gluckists is a bit disarming: in opera within opera, or opera about opera, we remain in the simple register of the *mise-en-abyme* and of citation; and in the end, we do not choose at all; with an emphatic wink we leave the generic conflict within opera in suspense. By contrast, in Berg (Wozzeck, the "poor creature," is the interdiction of eloquence, of music, and consequently is interdiction itself) and above all in Schönberg, the problem is touched upon at greater depth. And with a very different acuity.

Above all in Schönberg, it is well known that this problem is the very subject of *Moses and Aaron*, and, even more essential, that it is constitutive of the opera's treatment. The opposition of speech and singing (or more exactly, of *Sprechgesang* and *Gesang*), which, no matter what Adorno says, very rigorously transposes the biblical opposition of Moses' stammering and Aaron's eloquence into the register of opera—and here the very question of the prohibition of (re)presentation, which thus is *also* the subject of the opera, is condensed—leads the opera to put its own principle into question with great lucidity. And consequently to reopen the scar that Wagner, with musical saturation, had intended to suture definitively in a sort of hyperbolic assumption of opera. Yet what Adorno, who is in fact one of the few who have confronted Schönberg's *oeuvre désoeuvrée*, "saves" from *Moses*, despite his vigilance with regard to Wagnerism, is precisely musical saturation. In the final pages of his important essay of 1963, "A Sacred Fragment: On Schönberg's *Moses and Aaron*,"[3] Adorno remarks that Schönberg, who evidently does not order his work according to a dramaturgy of the Wagnerian type (if a traditional model is still operative, it would be that of oratorio). This prevents nothing: when Adorno wants to justify what he calls the "success" of *Moses*, what he brings forward is the work's "power," and does so all the more because this power accords with the metaphysical (or religious) aims of the work. Yet where does this power come from, or this "greatness of tone," which amounts to the same thing? Not from simplicity, at least not immediately, but rather "with everything which is gathered together in this music and which occupies the musical space" (p. 244). Adorno comments:

> In no other work does Schönberg so consistently and with such facility follow the rule that the compositional effort—that is to say, in the first place the sheer quantity of simultaneous events—should correspond to the content of the music, of the events to be represented. In *Moses* he takes this to extremes. Nowhere else is there so much music, almost in the literal sense of so many notes, as here *ad majorem Dei gloriam*. The sheer density of the construction becomes the medium in which the ineffable can manifest itself without usurpation. For it is this that can be wholly and convincingly created in the material by Schönberg's own musical consciousness. (pp. 244–45)

Once again the style of this saturation is not Wagnerian, if only because the writing is too complex and because it no longer orders itself according to the imperative of a *melos*. But all the same, it is saturation. And it is linked to a religious or metaphysical content as its most adequate mode of expression. It is as if, in the end, *Moses and Aaron* were nothing other than the negative (in the photographic sense) of *Parsifal*, thus accomplishing, in a paradoxical manner, the project of the total work. And in fact, this is virtually what we read in Adorno's final remarks:

> By conceptualizing this we have probably arrived at the full measure of Schönberg's success in his biblical opera. It is intensified by what seems at first to stand in its way: the inordinate complexity of the music. This leads to the liberation of Schönberg's supreme talent, his gift for combination, his precise grasp of distinct but simultaneous events. The idea of unity in diversity becomes a sensuous musical reality in him. He was able not just to imagine, but actually to invent complexes of opposed extremes, which yet occur simultaneously. In this respect he represents the culmination of the tradition in which every detail is composed. This talent reveals his metaphysical ingenuity. The unity of what he had imagined truly does justice to the idea which forms the subject of the text. The striking effect and the unity of the disparate are one and the same. Hence the simplicity of the end result. The complexity is nowhere suppressed, but is so shaped as to become

transparent. If everything in the score is clearly heard, its very clarity means that it is heard as a synthesis. (pp. 247–48)

With the exception of the clarity (and more . . .), we see that this description could apply to Wagner. In any case, the possibility of a "synthetic perception," the unified (and thus totalizing) nature of music, the adequation of such a unity to the "idea" of the text (to its metaphysical signification), the "obligation" itself, these are all incontestably principles that come from Wagnerian aesthetics. The question then arises, and it is not inconsequential: how is it that Wagner's shadow can still darken the hope, which was as much Schönberg's as Adorno's, of putting an end—lucidly—to Wagner-ism? Which is to say to the worst (the most disastrous) conception of "great art"?

If there is any chance of making sense of this, it will be in re-reading "A Sacred Fragment."

~

At the end of his analysis, that is, just before the Benjaminian *Rettung* of the work that neatly finishes the essay on Schönberg, we find this statement (Adorno, who without ever mentioning the word has catalogued the reasons for the failure of *Moses*, has just indicated that in the end Schönberg was the victim of the bour-geois illusion of "art's eternity," of the belief in genius—that meta-physical transfiguration of bourgeois individualism—indeed, of the absence of doubt as to the reality of greatness; or to put it oth-erwise, that he was the victim of his own renunciation of "that aes-thetic extremism, the sole legitimation of art," and he continues):

In Schönberg's fragmentary main works—the term 'main work' is symptomatic—there is something of the spirit that Huxley castigates in one of his early novels. The greatness, universal validity, totality of the masters and masterpieces of yore—all this can be regained if only you are strong enough and have the genius. This has something of the outlook that plays off Michelangelo against Picasso. Such blindness about the philosophy of history has causes rooted in the history of philosophy itself. They are to be found in the feeling of an inade-quate sense of authority, the shadow-side of modern individuation. To overcome this blindness would mean relativizing the idea of great art even though great art alone can provide the aesthetic seriousness in whose absence authentic works can no longer be written. Schönberg has actually rendered visible one of the antinomies of art itself. The most powerful argument in his favour is that he introduced this antinomy, which is anything but peculiar to him, into the innermost recesses of his own *oeuvre*. It is not to be overcome simply by an act of will or by virtue of the power of his own works. The fallacy that it is necessary to negotiate or depict the most rarefied contents in order to produce the greatest works of art—a fallacy which puts an end to the Hegelian aesthetics—derives from the same misconception. The elusive content is to be captured by chaining it to the subject matter which, according to tradition, it once inhabited. A futile endeavor. The prohibition on graven images which Schönberg heeded as few others have done, nevertheless extends further than even he imagined. To thematize great subjects directly today means projecting their image after the event. But this in turn inevitably means that, disguised as themselves, they fail to make contact with the work of art. (pp. 242–43; translation slightly modified)

Schönberg's merit, which however does not yet permit the "saving" of his work, is thus to have "brought an antinomy of art itself to the fore" (and not just, as one might think, an antinomy of the art of the "bourgeois era" and of the epoch of individuation, even if it has devolved upon properly modern art to manifest it). This antinomy is very simple, and is without resolution: "great art" is and cannot be (or can no longer be) the guarantee, indeed the norm, of authenticity in art. The notion of "great art," which alone founds "just that measure of aesthetic seriousness without which something authentic can no longer be written at all," must be "relativized." But one does not relativize the absolute. "Great art" remains the norm—just as, for reasons that are hardly different, it was for Hegel and Schelling, for Nietzsche, for Heidegger—but it is a ruinous norm for all art that would submit itself to this category. This is why "great art," the will to "great art," is the impossibility of art. This contradiction is at the very heart of Schönberg's work, and especially of *Moses*, and we will see that it is this that makes for its "greatness," beyond its "intention." In its *Wahrheitsgehalt*, as Benjamin said: in its truth content.

This is ultimately what defines the essence of art, at least of modern art: it is only itself in the impossibility of effectuating that which founds its authenticity. It does not follow from this that one must renounce "apprehending . . . the most rarefied contents" (the spiritual contents, as Hegel said, the metaphysical as such, for this is and has always been "the height"). But it does follow, on the other hand, that one must renounce "treating or presenting [*darstellen*] the highest contents." If one here credits Adorno with the greatest lucidity (and the allusion to Hegel cannot but lead one to do so), what is seen as the "error" is exactly what Heidegger, in the first version of his lectures on the "Origin of the Work of Art," denounced as the "remarkable fate" to which "all meditation on art and the artwork, all theory of art and aesthetics" was submitted, from the Greeks at least until Hegel, which is to say until us: the artwork "always *also* admits to being considered as a fabricated thing [*ein Zeugwerk*, an allusion to the Platonico-Aristotelian misinterpretation of *tekhnè*] which in addition presents a 'spiritual meaning.' Art is accordingly the representation of something supra-sensual in formed sensual matter."[4] However, this questioning of *Darstellung* (art is not *essentially* [re]presentation) is what Adorno refers, both because of Schönberg and beyond him, to the biblical interdiction of representation—to the "iconoclast prescription," as Jean-Joseph Goux calls it[5]—which "extends further even than Schönberg could imagine, who respected it as no one else did." It goes without saying that here all comparison with the Heideggerian procedure ends. If there is indeed something that Heidegger couldn't—or rather wouldn't—recognize, even if his thought and the deconstruction of Hegelian aesthetics ought to have forced him to do so, it is that one might refer the problematic of *Darstellung* to such an origin. But Adorno had every reason to do just this. And so it is that he affirms, in a mode that Heidegger would most probably have rejected, that of these "great contents," today—which leads us all the same to modern art, to the art made according to the art in which, traditionally, the content was attached to particular subjects—of these "great contents" it remains only to "conceive" the "trace." All of which amounts to saying "necessarily that they elude the work of art by their very nature." Here it is clear that we have touched on the problem of the "end of art." Since Hegel, the end of art has signified the birth of aesthetics (the philosophy or science of art, or even the simple "reflection" on art), no matter where one situates the event: in the decline of the Greek fifth century, as Heidegger above all would be tempted to think, or in the exhaustion of Christian art. (In the meantime, the question is relatively secondary: in both cases, the end of art means in reality the end of religion, and this is the essential point.) In his own way, Adorno remains faithful to this determination: no doubt there was once "great art," which is to say that "great contents" were only able to provide material for works of art. But that all that remains is to conceive the trace of this—and this makes all the difference—in no way suffices to define the program of an aesthetics. Simply because "great contents" do not essentially belong to the work of art. If the project of an aesthetics must be maintained—and it is well known that Adorno, perhaps against Heidegger, will resolutely devote himself to this—it will not be reduced to ending, as is the case in Hegel and also, though in a more complex fashion, in Heidegger, as a nostalgia for a religion. Which is to say a community.

This is why it is not at all a matter of indifference that this set of problems—at once very close to and very far from Heideggerian questions, but close at least in that it is the dominating closure of Hegelian aesthetics that is rejected—should thus present all the marks of a philosophical reflection on the essence, the history, and the destination of art even as it proceeds both very rigorously and very loyally in its interpretation of *Moses*. This is an artwork, and not just any artwork, both in its intentions and in what lies beyond its intentions, and in the failure or success of the two, which produces or at least allows one to create such a set of problems. All things being equal, Schönberg is for Adorno what Schiller, for example, is for Hegel, Wagner for the early Nietzsche, and Hölderlin for Heidegger: the offering of a work that explicitly thematizes the

question of its own possibility as a work—modern in this way—
and that thereby carries in itself, as its most intimate subject, the
question of the essence of art. Such works necessitate a philosophical decision as to the future of art or its chances today—which is
to say from now on. Schiller sanctions the end of art (its "death"),
but Wagner is the hope of a rebirth. And Hölderlin, always on
condition of not wanting to envision his final lack of occupation
[*désoeuvrement*], is the hope of an "other beginning."

Thus the question is to know exactly what *Moses and Aaron* offers to Adorno (to the continuing project of aesthetics).

The response to this question lies entirely within the title
Adorno gives to his essay: "A Sacred Fragment."

Despite the peremptory (and perhaps uselessly romantic) declaration that virtually opens the essay, according to which "everything is in piece, fragmentary, like the Tablets of the Law which
Moses smashed," this title is not justified solely by the fact that
Moses and Aaron is unfinished. This would hardly explain the fact
that, despite appearances, the simplest meaning of the word "fragment" is in the end not at all the meaning retained by Adorno.
The reference here to the Tablets is in reality not formal; it is even
less formalist, in the genre of a more or less subtle *mise en abyme*.
As it appears a bit further on, only the word "sacred" is able to ex-
plain the "fragment," and it is to the metaromantic speculation of
Benjamin that one must connect the following corrective:

> Important works of art are the ones that aim for an extreme; they are
> destroyed in the process and their broken outlines survive as the ci-
> phers of a supreme, unnameable truth. It is in this positive sense that
> *Moses und Aron* is a fragment and it would not be extravagant to at-
> tempt to explain why it was left incomplete by arguing that it could
> not be completed.

No doubt there is still something of the *mise en abyme* in this final
formula. But the *mise en abyme* is necessary here because it is nothing other than the effect of the *reflection* that structures *Moses and
Aaron*. And it is difficult to see how an art that takes itself as its

own object, being constrained to put its own possibility to the test, might escape from it.

The hermeneutic principle that Adorno follows—he is in this way Benjaminian—in fact necessitates a double reading.

On the one hand, he locates, as the very *intention* that presides over the work, what he calls the "fundamental experience" of *Moses*: that of heroism which is properly *metaphysical* (more so, it would seem, than that of "religious" heroism). In applying himself to the beginning of the *Pieces for Choir*, Opus 27: "Heroic are those who accomplish acts for which they lack courage," Adorno designates the subject of *Moses* as the pure contradiction of a (consequently impossible) task, the task of "being the mouth of the absolute." This task is defined in a strictly Hegelian manner, if one remembers the *Lectures on the Philosophy of Religion*, where Hegel says that Moses "over there" (in the Orient, I suppose) has only "the value of an organ." Moreover, "contradiction" is defined in the Hegelian lexicon as the contradiction of the finite and the infinite: the absolute—rather than God, for what is at stake in Schönberg's libretto is "thought" and not faith—evades finite beings, with which it is incommensurable.

[According to Moses,] to act as the mouthpiece of the Almighty is blasphemy for mortal man. Schönberg must have touched on this theme even before *Die Jakobsleiter*, when he composed a setting for Rilke's poem in the songs Opus 22: "All who attempt to find you, they tempt you / And they who thus find you, they bind you / to image and gesture." Thus God, the Absolute, eludes finite beings. Where they desire to name him, because they must, they betray him. But if they keep silent about him, they acquiese in their own impotence and sin against the other, no less binding, commandment to name him. They lose heart because they are not up to the task which they are otherwise enjoined to attempt. (pp. 225–26; translation slightly modified)

And it is moreover to this contradiction that Adorno attributes the exclamation of Moses that interrupts the music composed by Schönberg—that is to say, for Adorno, the work itself, which is thereby condemned to fragmentation:

At the end of Act II of the biblical opera, in the final sentence which has become music, Moses breaks down and laments, "O word, thou word that I lack." The insoluble contradiction which Schönberg has taken as his project and which is attested by the entire tradition of tragedy, is also the contradiction of the actual work. If it is obvious that Schönberg felt himself to be a courageous man and that he invested much of himself in Moses, this implies that he advanced to the threshold of self-knowledge about his own project. He must have grasped the fact that its absolute metaphysical content would prevent it from becoming an aesthetic totality. But by the same token he refused to accept anything less. (p. 226)

Yet this contradiction, which Adorno very oddly describes as "tragic" (I will return to this), is not simply the subject of the work. Adorno insists a great deal on this: it is indeed the contradiction of the work itself, that is, "the impossibility of an aesthetic totality whose existence depends on an absolute metaphysical content." Thus the essential, and not accidental, incompleteness of *Moses.* This incompleteness is inscribed, ultimately, in Moses' very first words, which Adorno also has no need to recall: "Unique / Eternal / Omnipresent / Invisible / And unrepresentable God."

But "tragic," Adorno remarks, is not appropriate. And at the same time, the structure of the *mise en abyme* (the impossibility that "the work reflects as properly its own") is insufficient, because too premeditated, to allow easy access to the work: "The impossibility which appears intrinsic to the work is, in reality, an impossibility which was not intended. It is well known that great works can be recognized by the gap between their aim and their actual achievement" (p. 226).

This is why, on the other hand, this time in regard to the "truth content"—to that very thing, Benjamin would say, that constitutes the work as an "object of knowledge"—Adorno invokes a second, more essential reason for the incompleteness of *Moses,* or for its impossibility. This reason is the end of art, that is, the end of the possibility of "great art":

The impossibility we have in mind is historical: that of sacred art today and the idea of the binding, canonical, all-inclusive work that

Schönberg aspired to. The desire to outdo every form of subjectivity meant that he had subjectively to create a powerful, dominant self amidst all the feeble ones. An immense gulf opens up between the trans-subjective, the transcendentally valid that is linked to the Torah, on the one hand, and the free aesthetic act which created the work on the other. This contradiction becomes fused with the one which forms the theme of the work and directly constitutes its impossibility. Theologians have complained that the designation of monotheism as "thought"—that is, something which is only subjectively intended—diminished the idea of transcendence in the text, since every thought is in a sense transcendental. Nevertheless, a truth manifests itself in this, however clumsily it is expressed: the absolute was not present in the work other than as a subjective intention—or idea, as the philosophers would say. By conjuring up the Absolute, and hence making it dependent on the conjurer, Schönberg ensured that the work would not make it real. (pp. 226–27)

Thus Adorno's thesis, if allowed to be briefly summarized: in its intention, *Moses* is a "sacred opera"; but because "a religious music cannot be *willed*" (p. 455) and because "the problematic character of a religious art that single-handedly tears itself free from its epoch" cannot efface itself (p. 456), *Moses* is in truth a "sacred fragment."

It is not my intention to critique this thesis. It is perfectly solid, and takes its authority from precise and reliable historical and sociological considerations. It is supported by extremely fine textual and musical analyses, and it has the weight of certitude. Nevertheless, I believe it is possible to put this thesis to the test of a category that is called, precisely, "aesthetic," but to which Adorno, at least here,[6] does not make the slightest allusion although everything in his text refers to it, and does so constantly: the category of the *sublime*.

If I was, perhaps, surprised that Adorno could describe as tragic the contradiction between the finite and the infinite, which according to him is the subject of *Moses*, this is because this contradiction in Hegel—and this contradiction as Adorno himself envisions it—is nothing other than that of "sublimity," which as we know defines the properly Jewish moment of religion.[7] Moreover, at least since Kant,[8] the Mosaic utterance (the Law, but above all the prohibition of representation) has been presented as the paradigm of the sublime utterance. And it is probably the case that since Michelangelo, if we correctly interpret what Freud wished to say, the *figure* of Moses, as paradoxical as this might seem, has been taken as the emblematic figure of the sublime. The sublime, in the tradition of the sublime, is overdetermined by the biblical reference. Yet all of this happens as if Adorno did not want to hear this discussed.

Here things necessarily take a turn: even though Adorno manifests the will to exceed the Hegelian determination of "great art," and consequently of the beautiful—of the sensual presentation adequate to a spiritual content, to an Idea, which is for Hegel the (Greek) truth of the (Jewish) sublime, that is, of the affirmation of the fundamental inadequation of the sensual and the Idea, or of the incommensurability of the finite and the infinite, whence the prohibition of representation precisely originates—and given that he sketches this gesture vis-à-vis Hegel and, before him, vis-à-vis the whole philosophical tradition since Plato, insofar as it imagines the beautiful as the *eidetic* apprehension of being (and Adorno has a very clear awareness, for example, of the "figurative character of all European art," including music, if only because of the invention of the *stilo rappresentativo* and of *musica ficta*), how is it that Adorno was unable to see or did not want to see that in reality Schönberg's endeavor expressly inscribes itself in the canonical tradition of the sublime? This would have in no way prevented him from producing the demonstration that he produces and that is incontestable because the contradiction of *Moses* is in fact incontestable. But this would have permitted him, perhaps, to reach another "truth" of *Moses* or to attempt a *Rettung* that would not be solely aesthetic, that is, imprisoned by the principle of adequation and obliged to judge the "failure" or "success" of the work solely from the viewpoint of the beautiful. That would be, definitively, to judge from the Hegelian point of view.

If there is no "critique" to be made, there is however a "reproach" to be offered. I would like to try briefly to explain myself.[9] We can begin over again with this: if Adorno were attentive to the problematic of the sublime—if he had remembered only that Kant gives the very prohibition of representation as the privileged example of the sublime—he could have maintained his analysis without any essential modifications.[10] In any case, it is the Hegel of the considerations on Judaism and sublimity who subtends Adorno's procedure here, whether he knows it or not, and these considerations presuppose the "Analytic of the Sublime." Thus with one stroke he could have returned to all the analyses of purportedly sublime works or works recognized as sublime that, since Kant and Schiller, have been generally in agreement in thinking that there is no possible sublime presentation—or, *a fortiori*, figuration—and thus in thinking that the question of the very possibility of a sublime art always arises, at least as long as we continue to define art by (re)presentation. To take an example that Adorno must have known, this is exactly the difficulty Freud encounters when, on the basis of Schillerian aesthetics (the essay "Grace and Dignity"), he tackles Michelangelo's figure of Moses; not only does he remain perplexed as to the meaning of the figure, but in fact he wonders whether in the end it is still art, that is, if it is "successful" (it is a "limit," he thinks).

At the same time, one cannot forget that, as regards Kant, leaving out that which arises from nature's sublime (and which poses altogether different problems), the only examples of the sublime given by the *Third Critique* are examples of sublime *utterances* (as has been traditional since Longinus), of which the most important are not poetic utterances but instead prescriptive utterances and more specifically prohibitions, precisely like the Mosaic Law. Thus Kant speaks of "abstract (or restrictive) representation," indeed of "negative representation." And because it also bears on representation or figuration, the Mosaic utterance, in its sublime simplicity (it is a purely negative commandment), is evidently an utterance we could call metasublime: it tells the truth of the sub-

lime in a sublime manner: that there is no possible presentation of
the metaphysical or of the absolute. *Mutatis mutandis*, this is a bit
like the exclamation "O word, you Word that I lack," which for
Adorno completes Schönberg's *Moses*. But above all, what we must
not forget, says Kant, that inasmuch as a "presentation of the sublime" can belong to the fine arts (and one can well imagine why he
remains extremely circumspect on this point), the only three
modes or genres that one can rigorously recognize as "sublime genres" are (sacred) oratorio, the didactic (that is, philosophical)
poem, and verse tragedy.[11]

Yet it is precisely these three genres of the art of the sublime—if
such a thing exists or can exist—that *Moses* brings together *jointly*,
for it is simultaneously oratorio ("sacred," as Adorno says), philosophical poem (whose subject is nothing less than the absolute itself), and tragedy in verse (to which I will now return). At least *if
we make an abstraction of the opera form*. And this is why I am rais-
ing the question as to whether Adorno, beyond his critique of the
opera as such, might not have been able to accede to another
"truth" of the work.

That *Moses* is an opera is particularly difficult to dispute. It even
has, from the dramaturgical point of view, all the faults of the
genre: among other things, I am thinking of the episode of wor-
shiping the Golden Calf, which Adorno considers admirable from
the viewpoint of musical composition, but which, in the style of
the "obligatory ballet" (in the second act, of course), lacks none of
the lascivious absurdity of the "Flower Maidens" of *Parsifal*. But it
is already less difficult to dispute that the dramaturgical principles
he obeys are those of the Wagnerian music-drama. Even if *Moses*
can be understood as an anti-*Parsifal* (which would thus retain the
essence of that against which it protests), it does not seem to me
that one could affirm without further consideration, as Adorno
does, that Schönberg has the same attitude toward the biblical text
that Wagner has toward the myths that he reelaborates, even if
Adorno's argumentation appears from the outset unimpeachable
and is difficult to find fault with. Adorno conducts his demonstration in the following manner:

With the vestiges of a naivety which is perhaps indispensible [Schön-berg] puts his trust in proven methods. Not that he is tempted to re-sort to formulae in order to revive or renew sacred music. But he does strive for a balance between the pure musical development and the de-sire for monumentality, much as Wagner has done. He too extended his critique of the musical theatre to the bounds of what was possible in his day. But at the same time he wanted the larger-than-life as evi-dence of the sacred. He deluded himself into believing that he would find it in myths. They are inaccessible to the subjective imagination that aspires to the monumental while suspending the traditional canon of forms which alone would create it. *Moses und Aron* is tradi-tional in the sense that it follows the methods of Wagnerian dra-maturgy without a hiatus. It relates to the biblical narrative in just the same way as the music of the *Ring* or *Parsifal* relate to their un-derlying texts. The central problem is to find musical and dramatic methods whereby to represent the idea of the sacred—that is to say, not a mythical but an anti-mythical event. (pp. 239–40)

There is no doubt that *Moses* represents a compromise, nor is it doubtful that, as Adorno emphasizes further on, the musical lan-guage that Schönberg wanted to enlist in the service of monu-mentality, subject to dramaturgical constraints that are contrary to it, is destroyed as such: "The new language of music, entirely renovated to its innermost core, speaks as if it were still the old one" (p. 241). And it is true that the "unified pathos" of the work, a pathos that hardly suits Moses—that is to say, "the specifically Jewish inflection" (p. 240)—causes the musical elaboration, be-cause of this external fact, to "disavow the over-specific idea of the work as a whole": "The aesthetic drive toward sensual expression works to the detriment of what that drive brings into being" (p. 241). Is the dramaturgical model on which Schönberg bases his work that of Wagner?

Adorno points out this contradiction: a mythical dramaturgy with antimythical aims is in fact a contradiction only under two conditions. On the one hand, the dramatic action must be of a mythical type, which is to say not that the myth must supply the material for the libretto but—this at least is the solution Wagner found—that the stage action, as well as the mythical units and signifiers, must be constantly musically overdetermined (hence, the *Leitmotive*). Which is not at all the case in Schönberg. (In other words, Schönberg no doubt aims for a "music-drama" in the broad sense of the term, but all the same he does not respect Wagnerian dramaturgy). And on the other hand, the opera must desire to be, as Adorno says, a "sacred opera," as *Parsifal* manifestly desired to be.

Now, it is exactly on this point that Schönberg's lucidity is greatest. His religious intentions, his search for a "great sacred art," are undeniable. Equally undeniable is his determination—indissolubly artistic, philosophical, and political while *Moses* was in progress— to write an anti-*Parsifal* (which ultimately imposed itself). However, he gave this up, and not just at any time, but precisely in 1933—on this point Adorno says what must be said—and not just in any way, though on this point Adorno's remarks seem too brief.

Perhaps it is the case that in all of his argumentation—and this would be at the very least my hypothesis—Adorno twice allows himself to get carried away: the first time by the Wagnero-Nietzschean determination of music-drama, conceived as "new tragedy" or as "modern tragedy," the second time by the Hegelian determination of tragedy.

Hegel defines tragedy, or more exactly the tragic scenario, as "the struggle of new gods against ancient gods."[12] This is obviously the kind of scenario that Adorno rediscovers in *Moses*: the struggle of monotheism, as he says, against the gods of the tribe. Now as this is also, *mutatis mutandis*, the Wagnerian scenario (that of the *Ring* or of *Parsifal*), it is easy to see how the assimilation of the two is possible. (And this was surely the case, in one way or another, for Schönberg. Even if his true subject lay elsewhere—for as Adorno sees very well, it had to do with the very possibility of art—the rivalry with Wagner, and with Wagnerism, weighed on him with too great a force. Here I must admit that I am allowing myself to be guided by the admirable film version of *Moses* by Jean-Marie Straub and Danièle Huillet, for I must acknowledge that it is their dramaturgical intuition that is decisive here: staging the first two acts, but not what remains of the third, in a Greek setting, even if it is, for this production, actually the Roman theater of Alba Fucense in the Abruzzi. In its original intention, in fact, *Moses* is a tragedy.)

But thinking that an identity of scenario implies an identity of function means making quite a leap. In the direct line of the Nietzsche of *The Birth of Tragedy*, but equally that of the Hegel who analyzes tragedy as a "religious" work of art (which is also to say a political work of art), Adorno imagines tragedy spontaneously from the starting point of the chorus, and the chorus as the bearer of "religion" itself, not so much as fervor or belief, but as being-in-community. The chorus is not the people, nor the representative of the people (of the spectators); but it is all the same the sign that tragedy is originally a common or communitarian work of art, that it is community in and through the work. That is, a work without an individual or singular subject. That all "great art" is ultimately the creation of a people—a dogma of German aesthetics from Hegel to Heidegger. And despite everything—I mean: despite "critical theory"—Adorno accepts this dogma right up to the moment in which it is revealed that the failure of a music that "extends a hand to the cult" (p. 228) with such force and determination, "to worship" has to do with the fact that such a music, notwithstanding the affirmation of the "obligatory character" of its content, fails in being "substantial" in the Hegelian sense, because it is too "willed." And art can only attain greatness if the subject that carries it is—Adorno of course does not say: the people, but: society. This is why ultimately Adorno condenses all the questions of *Moses* into this, transcendental, question: How is a music of worship even possible outside of any worship? That is to say also outside of any religious adherence or faith? But above all, outside of any (social) effect of worship? I will add here, without commentary, the two following sections:

> The impossibility of the sacred work of art becomes increasingly evident the more the work insists on its claim to be one without invoking the support of any outside authority. With the modesty characteristic of the greatest emotional integrity, Schönberg ventured into this realm. The objection that the individual is no longer capable of the subjective piety which the biblical story calls for misses the mark.

Bruckner was presumably a believer in an anachronistic sense and as musically inspired as any composer can be. Yet the Promised Land remained closed to him, and perhaps even to the Beethoven of the *Missa Solemnis.* The impossibility we are speaking of extends right into the objective preconditions of the form. Sacred works of art—and the fact that *Moses und Aron* was written as an opera does not disqualify it from being one—claim that their substance is valid and binding, beyond all yearning and subjective expression. The very choice of canonical biblical events implies such a claim. It is certainly implicit in the pathos of the music of *Moses und Aron,* whose intensity gives reality to a communal "we" at every moment, a collective consciousness that takes precedence over every individual feeling, something of the order of the togetherness of a congregation. Were it otherwise, the predominance of the choruses would scarcely be imaginable. Without this transindividual element or, in other words, if it were merely a case of what is known as religious lyric poetry, the music would simply accompany the events or illustrate them. The compulsion to introduce into the music a sense of its own intellectual situation, to organize it in such a way that it expressed the underlying foundation of the events described, in short, its high aesthetic seriousness forces it into a collective stance. It must of necessity extend a hand to the cult if it is not entirely to fail its own intention. But cultic music cannot simply be willed. Anyone who goes in search of it compromises the very concept. (pp. 227–28)

We may legitimately ask what produced the conception of this work in the light of such immense difficulties, which may be compared to those experienced twenty years before in connection with *Die Jakobsleiter.* It is not the product of that misconceived monumentality, that unlegitimated gesture of authority which marks so much of the pictorial arts of the nineteenth century, from Puvis de Chavannes down to Marées. Of course it was Schönberg's own individual make-up that provided the critical impetus. His parents do not seem to have been orthodox in their beliefs, but it may be supposed that the descendant of a family of Bratislava Jews living in the Leopoldstadt, and anything but fully emancipated, was not wholly free of that subterranean mystical tradition to be found in many of his contemporaries of similar origins, men such as Kraus, Kafka and Mahler.

The Enlightenment displaced the theological heritage, shifting it on to the plane of the apocryphal, as we can infer from Schönberg's

own autobiographical remarks. In particular, superstition survived
tenaciously in his life and he often reflected on it. It is doubtless an in-
stance of secularized mysticism. The experience of pre-fascist Germany, in which he rediscovered his Jewish roots, must have released
this repressed dimension of his nature. *Moses und Aron* was composed
directly before the outbreak of the Third Reich, probably as a defen-
sive reaction to what was about to sweep over him. Later, even after
Hitler's fall, he did not return to the score. (p. 232)

The fact that a question of the transcendental type is fundamental to *Moses* is unequivocal, and it would probably have been
difficult for it to be otherwise if one considers what regularly links
Kant to the figure of Moses in the German tradition ("Kant is the
Moses of our nation," said Hölderlin). But it is perhaps not so
certain that this question bears on the possibility of a sacred art in
the final analysis.

In reality Adorno's demonstration is only possible inasmuch as it
attaches itself almost exclusively to the music and remains perfectly indifferent to the rest, that is, to the text. A text that is not
reducible to the libretto but that rather suggests, beyond the scenario itself (in its strange loyalty to the biblical text, which Adorno
also greatly underestimates), the dramaturgical structures this scenario introduces (for example, the chorus, which is in fact the people, is not at all Greek and in no way has a relation of the tragic
type to the protagonists, despite immediate appearances) and,
above all, the poem. Yet not only does Adorno pay no attention to
the text of Act III, under the pretext that it is not set to music
(even so, this is decisive for the meaning that Schönberg expressly
wished to confer upon the work, which then concludes, as it is in
fact written, with the pardon—and death—of Aaron), but he also
systematically minimizes the problem of the relation between
thought and language, a relation that is central, by assigning it to
an inevitably subjective and profane ("heretical") interpretation of
revelation, even though it is perhaps here that the transcendental
question is articulated for Moses himself.

This essentially exclusive attention accorded to the music is verified in a privileged way in the final *Rettung*, which is entirely de-

voted to demonstrating the "success" of the work, which is to say its adequation, despite the fundamental contradiction between intention and composition that subtends the opera. All of which comes down to displaying an internal adequation of the musical texture itself (identified *in fine* with the final accomplishment, by way of musical genius, of the passage to monotheism),[13] which itself properly redeems the fault of making *musica ficta* serve against the figure. And it is such an adequation that fundamentally reestablishes, beyond the peripeteias of "great art" in the bourgeois era, the enigmatic but unseverable link between music and Jewishness.[14]

   At the same time, if one pays attention to the critical aspect of the analysis, this exclusive attention to the music is again what explains that besides the main grievance (music would be the image of what escapes from any image), one of the major accusations bears on the "unified pathos" of the work. As Adorno very clearly indicates, not only does the incrimination take aim at the "factitious" character of pathos, which arises because the religious content has lost all "substantiality," but further, as a result of this, the "new language," withdrawing from itself, "speaks as if it were still the old one" (p. 240), according to a compromise of the Wagnerian type between monumentality and musical modernity, which authorizes Adorno to speak of the strangely "traditional" effect of *Moses.* Nor does it take aim only at the insufficient differentiation of the couple formed by Moses and Aaron, the one who speaks and the one who sings, due this time to the "imitative" overdetermination of the music. Moses, says Adorno, should not speak, for in the Bible he stutters. He adds that "it highlights the crisis of an art which makes use of this text purely as art and of its own free will" (p. 230). But further, it essentially aims for obedience to the Wagnerian principle of the unity of language, which "cannot accommodate what the subject matter requires above all: the strict separation of Moses' monotheism from the realm of myth, the regression to the tribal gods. The pathos of the music is identical in both" (p. 241). And it is here, moreover, that Adorno puts his fundamental hermeneutic principle into play, one that is borrowed once again from Benjamin, this time from the Benjamin of the very celebrated essay titled "Goethe's *Elective Affinities.*" For Adorno explains that if one wishes to break the "vicious circle" of "entrapment in the coils of myth" that alone justifies the unity of language and technique in Wagner, "the caesura was to be decisive." But, he remarks, "the rupture was to become music" (p. 241). This is evidently not the case:

> The undifferentiated unity from which the ruthless process of the integration allows nothing to be exempted comes into collision with the idea of the One itself. Moses and the Dance round the Golden Calf actually speak the same language in the opera, although the latter must aim to distinguish between them. This brings us close to the source of traditionalism in Schönberg, an issue which has only started to become visible in recent decades and especially since his death. In his eyes the idea of musical vocabulary as the organ of meaning was still instinctive and unquestioned. This vocabulary imagined itself able to articulate everything at any time. But this assumption was shaken by Schönberg's own innovations. (pp. 241–42)

In other words, Schönberg betrays his own modernism. He uses the codified syntax of tonality as a base, even though his atonality would order that he break it, in conformity with the subject of the work (which would thus be, one must believe: how is it that only atonal music is adequate to the monotheistic idea?). Because of this, Schönberg would be a victim of his epoch, exactly as Schiller was for Hegel. He would succumb to the bourgeois idea of genius, which is to say—but Adorno, precisely, does not say this and probably could not, at least not as crudely—of the sublime. But nevertheless, this is what is at stake; the lexicon is not misleading:

> This introduces a fictional element into the actual construction which so energetically opposes one. The situation points back to an illusion from which the bourgeois spirit has never been able to free itself: that of the unhistorical immortality of art. It forms a perfect complement to that decorative stance from which the Schönbergian innovations had effected their escape. The belief in genius, that metaphysical transfiguration of bourgeois individualism, does not allow any doubt to arise that great men can achieve great things at any time and that

the greatest achievements are always available to them. No doubt can be permitted to impugn the category of greatness, not even for Schön-berg. A justified scepticism towards that belief, which is based on a naive view of culture as a whole, is to be found in that specialization which Schönberg rightly opposed on the grounds that it acquiesced in the division of labor and renounced that extreme of the aesthetic, the sole legitimation of art. (p. 242)

A verdict without appeal, but which is all the same astonishing from someone who bases his work on the *past* existence of a "great sacred art" in order to condemn any and all factitious "restora-tions," as if at the same time, to put it by way of a shortcut, the sublime (grandeur) were a bourgeois invention and "great sacred art" were not a retrospective illusion—a projection—of the edu-cated German bourgeoisie from Hegel to Heidegger, or from Kant to Adorno himself. That "aesthetic extremism" should be "the sole legitimation of art," for us, today, is not doubtful. Who knows if this was not also the case for Sophocles, or for Bach? And who knows if it is not precisely this that Wagner betrayed with his "compromises," but not Schönberg, who, as a victim of the bour-geois mythology of art—as Adorno is right to emphasize—all the same chose to abandon (one can suppose: know full well the cause of his decision) *Moses*, to *interrupt* it, rather than present supple-mentary evidence for the remythologization of art and of religion.

~

In any case, the question remains: what exactly does Adorno mean when he declares that the rupture (or the caesura) itself should have made "itself music"? It is easy to see that what is in-criminated here is the too powerful homogeneity of the music, the flawless density that paradoxically (or rather dialectically) "re-deems" or "saves" it as music to the detriment of the work itself in its project, that is, as a "sacred opera." The opposition of the *Sprechgesang* and the *melos*, to put it another way, does not "caesure" the continuity of the musical discourse, nor therefore does it bring out the monotheistic idea. The unity of language is pagan, idola-trous. But is the caesura simply a matter of differentiation internal to language? Or even of the clear-cut opposition of voices? In what sense, ultimately, does Adorno understand "caesura"? And, as part of the same question: why does he make so little of the interruption of the work—apparently accidental, "empirical," but will we ever know—and, above all, why does he make so little of the very strange mode in which this interruption comes about? In no way do I wish to suggest that the interruption *is* the caesura, but perhaps that the caesura, more inaudible to Adorno's ear than it is invisible to his eyes, is hidden in the interruption—which, from then on, would no longer be thinkable as interruption.

Here of course we must give credit to Adorno for using, in a manner analogous to that which he uses with the word *Rettung*, the word *caesura* in the broader but rigorous sense that Benjamin gives it in his essay on Goethe, where it identified as the technical term forged by Hölderlin for his structural theory of tragedy and elevated to the level of a general critical (or aesthetic) concept: all works are organized as such from the starting point of the caesura inasmuch as the caesura is the hiatus, the suspension, or the "antirhythmic" interruption that is not only a necessity, as in metrics, for the articulation and the equilibrium of verse (of the phrase and, by extension, of what one might call the work-phrase), but also, more essentially, the place from which what Hölderlin calls "pure speech" emerges. The caesura, to put it otherwise, is the liberation by default—but a non-negative default—of meaning itself or of the truth of the work. And from the critical point of view, it is only the caesura that indicates, in the work, the place that one must reach in order to accede to the *Wahrheitsgehalt*.[15]

On the basis of this hermeneutic model, Adorno is right to look for the caesura in *Moses*, as in any supposedly great work. Perhaps his only fault is looking for it, through "melocentrism," only in the music. For if one takes stock of what Schönberg effectively *wrote*, one can just as well construct the hypothesis that it is at the very place where the music—but not the work—is interrupted, that is, precisely where Moses proclaims that the word (speech) fails him: *O Wort, du Wort, das mir fehlt!*

In fact, we know that up until this end of the second act, Schönberg composed the libretto and the score *simultaneously*. And that at the moment when he was to begin composing the third act—whether the cause was accidental or not does not matter here—abruptly and without giving any indication of exactly why, he only wrote the text of one scene, the scene where Moses, reaffirming his "idea," pardons Aaron, or at least orders that he not be executed. And here again it must be noted that the dramaturgical choice of Straub and Huillet is especially illuminating: for not only do they play this scene—spoken only—in the unbearable silence that succeeds the unfurling of the music, a silence that Adorno analyzes so well, but they also set it in another place than that which, from the outset, constituted the stage or theater. They do this in such a way that it is not only the tragic mode, as Adorno understands it, that collapses in a single stroke, but the entire structure that kept *Moses* within the frame of opera or music drama. And it is here, in all probability, that religion is interrupted.

If such an idea is right; if, dramaturgically, one must account for this rupture or this hiatus and the passage to simple speech—for such is the enigma of what remains of Schönberg's work—then there is indeed caesura, and it sheds a different light on the truth of the work. In particular, it no longer permits one to link the difference in enunciation between the two protagonists to Schönberg's submission to the imperatives of *musica ficta* (and of Wagnerian dramaturgy). That difference starts from the principle that the music must be swallowed up and that only the naked word remain.

Beyond its structural function, in Hölderlin the caesura signifies—and it is because of this that it holds Benjamin's attention—the interruption *necessary* for tragic truth to appear, which is to say the necessary separation, the necessary break that must (but in the sense of a *Sollen*) be produced in the process of infinite collusion between the human and the divine, which is the tragic flaw itself, *hubris.* The tragic separation, the uncoupling of God and man (which Hölderlin interprets as *katharsis*), thus signifies the law of finitude, which is to say the impossibility of the immediate: "For mortals just as for immortals, the immediate is prohibited." There is no more possibility of an immediate interpretation of the divine (Oedipus) than there is of an immediate identification with the divine (Antigone). Mediation is the law (*Gesetz*), a law, moreover, that Hölderlin conceives in a rigorously Kantian fashion (as when he speaks of the "categorical diversion" of the divine, which brings about the imperative obligation for man to return toward the earth.[16]

From here on, according to this model—and according to the logic of the extension of the concept inaugurated by Benjamin and apparently recognized by Adorno himself—why should we not think that insofar as it marks and suspends the music in the course of a brief and dry scene, the caesura in *Moses* brutally makes it appear that Moses, the inflexible guardian of the Law and the defender of his own great—his own sublime—conception of God, is also the one who by virtue of immoderation wants to be the too immediate interpreter of God: the mouth or the organ of the absolute, the very voice of God as its truth. This is why in never ceasing to proclaim the unrepresentability of God, indeed his ineffability, neither will he cease (on the same terrain of *musica ficta* where Aaron operates with great ease) striving to sing and not to confine himself strictly to speech, as if, by the effect of a compromise induced by his rivalry with Aaron, he were secretly tempted by the idea of a possible presentation (a sublime presentation, according to the rules of his great eloquence) of the true God, of the unpresentable itself. To the point where, for lack of speech or a word, in the despairing recognition of this lack—and here, precisely at this phrase the caesura is situated—he is swallowed up by his own great audacity and the music is interrupted. By this one may understand why, in the only scene of the final act—all "sobriety" as Hölderlin would have said—Moses grants his pardon, which is to say he repudiates murder. Thus is verified the profound insight that underlies Freud's *Moses and Monotheism*, according to which the prohibition of representation is nothing other than the prohibition of murder.[17]

Such is the reason why that which is interrupted along with the music, that which is "caesuraed," is religion itself, if religion is defined as the belief in a possible (re)presentation of the divine, that is, if religion is unthinkable without an art or as an art (which, fortunately, does not mean—"holding the line"—that art would be unthinkable without religion or as religion). What is at stake here, in the interruption of what was without a doubt at the outset the project of a "sacred opera," is the very thing Adorno considers to be beyond doubt for Schönberg: the figurativity of music. But in order to recognize this, it would have been necessary for Adorno to consider *reading Moses*, and not simply hearing it. Or it would have been necessary perhaps for him to be able to recognize, in according more credit (or trust) to Schönberg, the limits of his own musical mysticism.

At one moment in his analysis, Adorno notes this:

> Schönberg's own need to express is one that rejects mediation and convention and therefore one which names its object directly. Its secret model is that of revealing the Name. Whatever subjective motive lay behind Schönberg's choice of a religious work, it possessed an objective aspect from the very outset—a purely musical one in the first instance. (p. 233)

But it is not the same Adorno who had written some years earlier:

> The language of music is quite different from the language of intentionality. It contains a theological dimension. What it has to say is simultaneously revealed and concealed. Its Idea is the divine Name which has been given shape. It is demythologized prayer, rid of efficacious magic. It is the human attempt, doomed as ever, to name the Name, not to communicate meanings.[18]

For Adorno, as for Schönberg, music in its very intention would, in short, come under the horizon of what Benjamin called "pure language,"[19] which is perhaps not without a relation to what Hölderlin, on the subject of the caesura, called "pure speech." But the Name, as Adorno well knows, is unpronounceable—and music is a vain prayer, the sublime as such, according to its most tried and true code since Kant: "All music has for its Idea the form of the divine Name." An art (of the) beyond (of) signification, which is to say (of the) beyond (of) representation. All the same, under the *O*

Wort, du Wort, das mir fehlt! that Moses proclaims in the last burst of music, one is not prohibited from hearing the resonation of an *O Name, du Name, der mir fehlt!* As when Kant takes as his major example of the sublime utterance the very prohibition of representation (the Mosaic law), this is in reality a metasublime utterance that tells in a sublime manner—and the passage to the naked word in Act III of *Moses* is absolutely sublime—the truth of the sublime, itself sublime. Ultimate paradox: the naked word—the language of signification itself—comes to tell of the impossible beyond of signification, something that Benjamin would not have denied. And to signify the transcendental illusion of expression. This is why *Moses* is not "successful." It is "unsavable" if for Adorno "to save" never means anything other than to consider artworks according to the scale of adequation, which is to say, of beauty: the religious gesture par excellence. Yet what *Moses* says precisely but despite itself—and one must well imagine Schönberg constrained and forced, which is after all the lot of every modern artist—is that art is religion at the limit of simple inadequation. Probably the end, in every sense, of religion. Or to be more precise: the caesura of religion.[20]

Notes

Preface

1. Philippe Lacoue-Labarthe, *La Fiction du politique* (Paris: Bourgois, 1987), translated as *Heidegger, Art and Politics: The Fiction of the Political*, trans. Chris Turner (Oxford: Blackwell, 1990).

Chapter 1: Baudelaire

1. Except when noted, all translations are my own.—Trans.
2. The French is *reconnaissance*, which means both "recognition" and "gratitude."—Trans.
3. *Selected Letters of Charles Baudelaire*, trans. and ed. Rosemary Lloyd (Chicago: University of Chicago Press, 1986), pp. 145–46. [Translation slightly modified.—Trans.]
4. Here I am taking up an expression that I have already used to translate and comment upon the title of the book by Theodor Reik, *The Haunting Melody*. I will take the liberty of referring to my essay "L'Écho du sujet," in *Le Sujet de la philosophie* (Paris: Aubier-Flammarion, 1979).
5. The French text was Richard Wagner, *Quatre poèmes d'opéra*, prefaced by his "Lettre sur la musique," republished by Mercure de France, 1941. Subsequent quotations of Wagner's "Lettre" will be from this edition and will be cited in text by page number.
6. Here I am referring to the work of Gérard Genette and Peter Szondi in general. Also to Philippe Lacoue-Labarthe and Jean-Luc Nancy, *L'Absolu littéraire* (Paris: Le Seuil, 1978).
7. Baudelaire, *Oeuvres complètes*, ed. Claude Pichois (Paris: Gallimard,

Bibliothèque de la Pléiade, 1976), 2: 120. [Further citations of this source will give only volume and page numbers, without mentioning the title.—Trans.]

8. See Lucien Braun, "La Music au centre (Herder)," in *Musique et philosophie* (Strasbourg: Cahiers du Séminaire de philosophie, Presses Universitaires de Strasbourg, 1987).

9. This has been a political problematic, if not *the* political problematic, of Germany since the eighteenth century. As I have tried to show elsewhere (in my *L'Imitation des modernes* [Paris: Galilée, 1986] and *La Fiction du politique* [Paris: Bourgois, 1987]), the question of art, that is to say the question of the possibility of a *German* art, is inscribed in a mimetic logic (rivalry with the "Romanesque" culture, and the French in particular, agonistic imitation of Greece). Its echo is heard in the French reactions to Wagner, discretely in Baudelaire, but much more clearly in Mallarmé.

10. I am borrowing this term from Roland Barthes, who himself claimed to have it from Benvéniste.

11. See Lacoue-Labarthe, *L'Imitation des modernes*.

12. I say "naively" because Wagner does not make explicit the fundamental opposition that orders his demonstration here and that in reality will end up being fixed as the opposition between the Dionysiac and the Apollonian.

13. This is a metaphysical postulate received by Wagner. It derives from Schopenhauer and even from the earlier figures Rousseau and Herder. But we must not forget that he also has the security of Hegel, for whom music is the art of subjective interiority, the pure expression of the soul. This is perhaps what explains the relationship that one can establish between what I have called, in "L'écho du sujet," autobiographical compulsion and musical haunting, by which is indicated that in the constitution of *literature* as such, there is the possibility of subjective appropriation. Again Rousseau, who, in the ordeal of the pure loss of self, nevertheless invents, with the *Rêveries*, lyrical prose, where literature already, soberly, falls into an abyss.

14. It is in fact from Daniel Jenisch (*Geist und Charakter des achtzehnten Jahrhunderts* [Berlin, 1800], 3 vol.) that Herder gets this idea that "the success of modern music owes nothing, even in a distant way, to the Ancients: because among the poetic or plastic arts, there is not one that is as original and neo-European [*neueuropäisch-original*]) as our music. Here the genius, left on its own and without the possibility of referring

to a classical model, had to draw everything from himself" (I, p. 429; cited by Braun in "La musique au centre [Herder]").

15. Wagner writes: "If we consider with attention the history of the development of languages, we perceive even today, in the roots of words, an origin from which it clearly results that, in principle, the formation of the idea of an object coincided in a nearly complete manner with the personal sensation that it caused us; and perhaps it is not so ridiculous to admit that the first human language must have had a great resemblance with song" ("Lettre sur la musique," pp. 57–58). This is the mark of a fundamental "Cratylism"—and consequently of the etymologism, common to all (post-Rousseauist) romantic linguistics. Such a view of language is also the principle of the poetic writing of Wagner and of the phrasing of his recitatives.

16. Such is, among other examples, the conclusion of Schelling's *System of Transcendental Idealism* of 1800.

17. Baudelaire, *Fusées*, XIII (in 1: 662): "Créer un poncif, c'est le génie. / Je dois créer un poncif." ["To create a pattern, that is genius. / I must create a pattern." A "poncif" is the name given to a pounced drawing, and figuratively to a banal or conventional work.—Trans.]

18. The anti-Semitism is proclaimed and public in Wagner; more secret, but not less "radical," in Baudelaire. We know this concise aesthetico-political program: "Belle conspiration à organiser pour l'extermination de la Race Juive" (*Mon coeur mis à nu*, in 1: 706).

19. See Lacoue-Labarthe, *La Fiction du politique*.

20. Fritz Stern, *Politique et désespoir (Le ressentiments contre la modernité dans l'Allemagne préhitlérienne)*, French translation by Catherine Malamoud (Paris: Armand Colin, 1990), p. 155.

21. Baudelaire, *Richard Wagner and "Tannhäuser" in Paris*, in *Selected Writings on Art and Literature*, trans. P. E. Charvet (London: Penguin Books, 1992), p. 325. [Further citations of *Selected Writings* will give Charvet's name and the page number. In a few passages, Charvet's translations have been slightly modified.—Trans.]

22. The first strophe, at any rate, is very clear:

> La musique souvent me prend comme une mer!
> Vers ma pâle étoile,
> Sous un plafond de brume ou dans un vaste éther,
> Je mets à la voile.
> (Baudelaire, 1: 68)

> Music often takes me like a sea!

Toward my pale star,
Under a ceiling of fog or in a vast ether,
I set to sail.

23. Baudelaire, trans. Charvet.

24. Baudelaire, 2: 165. Here again it is a matter of a common site issuing from eighteenth-century linguistics and from the first romanticism.

25. Here I will take the liberty of referring to my "La Verité sublime," in Jean-François Courtine et al., *Du sublime* (Paris: Belin, 1987); translated as *Of the Sublime: Presence in Question*, trans. Jeffrey S. Librett (Albany: State University of New York Press, 1993).

26. See Jean-Luc Nancy, "L'Offrande sublime," in Courtine et al., *Du sublime.*

27. Baudelaire, after recalling how Wagner laid claim to Greek tragedy, insists strongly on the "legendary" character of Wagner's libretti and cites at length the arguments that the "Letter on Music" devotes to myth (2: 789ff.). But to stress this, it is true, is also to credit Wagner with being a great critic: "How would Wagner not understand admirably the sacred, divine character of myth, he who is at once poet and critic?" (2: 792).

28. "No musician excels as Wagner does in *painting* material and spiritual space and depth. . . . It seems sometimes, in listening to this ardent and despotic music, that we find painted on the background of shadows, torn by reverie, the vertiginous conceptions of opium" (2: 785).

29. Baudelaire, trans. Charvet, pp. 342–43.

30. Walter Benjamin, *Le Concept de critique esthétique dans le romantisme allemand*, trans. Philippe Lacoue-Labarthe and Anne-Marie Lang (Paris: Flammarion, 1986), pp. 150ff.

31. Baudelaire, trans. Charvet, p. 342.

32. See Jacques Derrida, *Psyché (Inventions de l'autre)* (Paris: Galilée, 1987).

33. Liszt, cited in Baudelaire, trans. Charvet, p. 350.

34. I will permit myself here to refer to my essay "Typographie," in Sylviane Agacinski et al., *Mimesis des articulations* (Paris: Aubier-Flammarion, 1975).

Chapter 2: Mallarmé

1. Mallarmé, "Solennité," in his *Crayonné au théâtre*, in Stéphane Mallarmé, *Oeuvres complètes*, Edition de la Pléiade, ed. Henri Mondor and G. Jean-Aubry (Paris: Gallimard, 1945), p. 335. [Further quotations

from works in the *Oeuvres* will be cited by page number, without mention of the latter title. All translations of Mallarmé are mine and are not definitive.—Trans.]

2. Mallarmé, "Richard Wagner: Rêverie d'un poète français," pp. 541–42. [This essay will be cited as "Reverie" below.—Trans.]

3. Mallarmé, "Hérésies artistiques.—L'Art pour tous," in *Proses de jeunesse*, p. 257.

4. Mallarmé, "Villiers de l'Isle-Adam," in *Quelques médaillons et portraits en pied*, p. 507.

5. These citations are from, respectively, the following essays in *Variations sur un sujet*: "Bucolique," p. 404; "Le Mystère dans les lettres," p. 385; and "Le Livre, instrument spirituel," p. 381.

6. Mallarmé, "Crise de vers," in *Variations sur un sujet*, p. 365.

7. Alain Badiou, "Est-il exact que toute pensée émet un coup de dés?," *Les Conférences du Perroquet*, no. 5 (Jan. 1986); and idem, *L'Être et l'événement* (Paris: Le Seuil, 1988).

8. Mallarmé, "Le Genre ou Des modernes," in *Crayonné au théâtre*, p. 312.

9. The French "historiale" suggests both *historique*, historical, and *historié*, used to describe figurative or figural art: "*Arts.* Décoré de scènes à personnages." *Le Petit Robert dictionnaire de la langue Française* (Paris, 1985), p. 932.—Trans.

10. Mallarmé, "Catholicisme," in *Variations sur un sujet*, p. 393.

11. Mallarmé, "De même," in *Variations sur un sujet*, p. 397.

12. Mallarmé, "Plaisir sacré," in *Variations sur un sujet*, p. 390.

13. Mallarmé, "Magie," in *Variations sur un sujet*, p. 399.

14. In "Le Genre ou Des modernes," the "pretension of the ill-bred . . . to some solemnization of the God that he knows to be" (p. 314) is a strictly undecidable proposition: is this God the God whom the ill-bred knows to exist? Or the God that the ill-bred, himself, knows himself to be? In the same way, in "Catholicisme," we find the expression: "the Divinity who is never but oneself" (p. 391). The secret of Mallarméan theology is perhaps held in this genre of undecidability.

15. "Solennité" (p. 330): "But where appears, as I exhibit regarding *dandysme*, my incompetence on anything other than the absolute . . . ?"

16. Mallarmé, "Plaisir sacré": "The poet, verbal, defies himself, he persists, in a nice prevention, by narrowness, but his supremacy in the name of the means, the consequently most humble essential, the word; however, at whatever height the chords and the brass exult, a verse, by the fact of its immediate approach to the soul, attains it" (p. 389).

17. Jean-Luc Nancy, *La Communauté désoeuvrée* (Paris: Christian Bourgois, 1986).

18. Mallarmé, "Catholicisme," p. 392. In "De même," Mallarmé says again: "Let us consider also that nothing, despite the insipid tendency, will be shown to be exclusively lay, because this word does not precisely elicit a sense" (p. 397).

19. Mallarmé, "De même," p. 396. "Egalitarian" sounds here, in these sentences, like a religious prescriptive—even a political one. It would be necessary to begin, on this motif, an analysis that I cannot develop in the framework I have fixed here. But I refer the reader to the most recent hypotheses—to the *tremblement* of the most recent hypotheses—offered by Alain Badiou on this subject ("L'outrepassement politique du philosophème de la communauté").

20. See my "Typographie," in Sylviane Agacinski et al., *Mimesis des articulations* (Paris: Aubier-Flammarion, 1975).

21. Jacques Derrida, *La Dissémination* (Paris: Le Seuil, 1972), pp. 248ff.

22. I forged this term "onto-typology" in "Typographie" on the model of the Heideggerian philosopheme of "onto-theology" to designate the ontology that underlies at once the most ancient thought of mimesis and the modern thought about figures (*Gestalt*) that proceeds from it. Cf., on this subject, Heidegger, *Contribution to the Question of Being*, trans. William Kluback and Jean T. Wilde (New Haven, Conn.: College and University Press, 1958).

23. Mallarmé, "Hamlet," in *Crayonné au théâtre*, p. 300.

24. Mallarmé, "Ballets," in *Crayonné au théâtre*, p. 306.

25. Mallarmé, "Crayonné au théâtre," in *Crayonné au théâtre*, pp. 295–96.

26. I will return in the following chapter to this properly metaphysical determination, according to Heidegger, of art.

27. Mallarmé, "Le Seul, il le fallait fluide . . . ," in *Crayonné au théâtre*, p. 312.

28. This solecism comes from Walter Benjamin, who, in his thesis on German romanticism, forged the neologism "das Musische" apropos of the Goethean theory of art, moreover without forcing the German. (See Benjamin, *Le Concept de critique esthétique dans le romantisme allemande*, trans. A.-M. Lang and Ph. Lacoue-Labarthe [Paris: Flammarion, 1986], pp. 165ff.) I owe the idea for undertaking such a translation to Giorgio Agamben.

29. Mallarmé, "Le Genre ou Des modernes," pp. 313–14. [The French misidentifies this citation as deriving from "Parenthèse," in *Crayonné au théâtre*, p. 324.—Trans.]

30. Mallarmé, "Rêverie," p. 546. By reason of the punctuation, the "Genius! me" is remarkably equivocal. As to the "minutes marked by solitude," they descend directly from Baudelaire.

31. Mallarmé's *La Music et les lettres*, for example, distinguishes England and France, among the nations, for having been the only ones to show, up until then, "a superstition for literature" (p. 643).

32. Mallarmé, *La Musique et les lettres*, p. 645.

33. Mallarmé, "Sur le théâtre," in *Proses diverses*, pp. 875–76. [The French *représentation* is rendered here and in the following paragraph of commentary in its theatrical meaning as "performance."—Trans.]

34. Mallarmé, "Rêverie," pp. 544–45. Evoking the "Ritual of one of the acts of Civilization," Mallarmé adds, as a note, "Exhibition, Transmission of Power, etc., I see you there, Brünhild or what would you do there, Siegfried!"

35. "Vain," placed by Mallarmé in quotation marks, leaves us unable to know if it refers to the interpretation or the fable. Both, no doubt, but also more likely the fable, because it is *empty* of all content.

36. Mallarmé, "L'Action restreinte," in *Variations sur un sujet*, p. 371.

37. "Planches et feuillets," "L'Action restreinte," "Le Livre, instrument spirituel," etc.

38. This is a constant definition in Mallarmé's writing: which explains that poetry is "the first and the last of the Arts" ("Solennité," p. 334).

39. Among other examples, we can read here in "Planches et feuillets": "*Pelléas et Mélisande* on a stage exhales, from pages, delight. To specify? These scenes, in brief, supreme: whatever is preparatory and machinelike has been rejected, in view of which seems, extract, what in a spectator is detached from the presentation, the essential. It seems that a superior variation on the admirable old melodrama is played. Almost silently and abstractly to the point that in this art, where everything becomes music in the proper sense, the part of an instrument that is itself pensive, the violin, will drown, by uselessness" (p. 330).

40. "Le Livre, instrument spirituel": "A solitary tacit concert is given, by reading, to the mind that takes over, on the least sonority, the signification: no mental means exalting the symphony, will miss, rarefied and that is all—by fact of thought. Poetry, near the Idea, is Music, par ex-

cellence—accepts no inferiority" (pp. 380–81). It goes without saying that the *instrument spirituel* is the truth, by purification, of all instrumentation.

41. The long-lived success of Fabre d'Olivet's book *Les Vers dorés de Pythagore expliqués* in the nineteenth century is well known. And of the many other texts of the same genre, that is to say, on mysticism or aesthetic esoterism (even aesthetico-political), which are visibly present in the Mallarméan conception of art and of religion—of art as religion.

42. Heidegger, translating "Archiloque," came to translate *rhuthmos* as *Ver-hältnis* (*rap-port*). See Roger Munier, "Rimbaud vivant," in Munier's *Aujourd'hui, Rimbaud . . .* (Paris: Archives des Lettres Modernes, 1976).

43. This quotation is from Mallarmé, *La Musique et les lettres*, p. 643.

44. Mallarmé, "Étalages," in *Variations sur un sujet*, p. 375.

Chapter 3: Heidegger

1. Among the most enlightening texts on this subject, see Bernard Baas, "L' 'Animal musicien' (Philosophie et musique chez Leibniz)," *Musique en jeu*, no. 25 (1976). [The translation cited in this chapter's epigraph is from Martin Heidegger, "Memorial Address," in his *Discourse on Thinking*, trans. John M. Anderson and E. Hans Freund (New York: Harper & Row, 1966), pp. 43–44.—Trans.]

2. The word, as I have already indicated in the chapter on Mallarmé, is borrowed from Benjamin; the French transcription proposed by Giorgio Agamben is *Musaïque*.

3. I have sketched this demonstration in my essay "Typographie," in Sylviane Agacinski et al., *Mimesis des articulations* (Paris: Aubier-Flammarion, 1975).

4. Martin Heidegger, "The Age of the World Picture," in *"The Question Concerning Technology" and Other Essays*, trans. William Lovitt (New York: Garland, 1977), pp. 142–43. [Translation slightly modified.—Trans.]

5. Martin Heidegger, *Nietzsche; Volume 1*, translated from the German by David Farrell Krell (San Francisco: Harper & Row, 1979). Heidegger's teaching on Nietzsche took place from 1936 to 1941. In what follows, I am principally referring to the first course (1936–37): "The Will to Power as Art," published in the first volume. [Lacoue-Labarthe here cites the French translation by P. Klossowski, mentioned in the text below.—Trans.]

6. 1962 for the French translation, which immediately produced a considerable effect. We know to what extent the Nietzschean question dominated the French philosophical scene up to the end of the 1970's.

7. But we should not forget that what this repetition must repeat— according to the logic developed apropos of the reading of Kant—is the unexpected, that is to say also the unthought and the unknown, in the beginning itself, which forever "passes over our heads," the most proper form of the *à-venir* [that which is to come; the future—Trans.].

8. See Jacques Derrida, "Le retrait de la métaphore," *Psyche (Inventions de l'autre)* (Paris: Galilée, 1987); Philippe Lacoue-Labarthe and Jean-Luc Nancy, "Ouverture," in Luc Ferry et al., *Rejouer le politique* (Paris: Galilée, 1981), and "Le 'retrait' du politique," in Jacob Rogozinski et al., *Le Retrait du politique* (Paris: Galilée, 1982).

9. "Truth of" is, however, not "identity with," even if it could be, up to a certain point, "solidarity (even complicity) with." Declaring Heidegger, in his thinking, uniformly *Nazi* obscures everything. Even an analysis as penetrating as that of Nicolas Tertullian on the (necessary) political translation of the principal Heideggerian philosophemes concerning the *Seinsgeschichte* ("Histoire de l'être et révolution politique— Réflexions sur un ouvrage posthume de Heidegger," *Les Temps modernes*, no. 523 [Feb. 1990]) cannot avoid doing so.

10. See my *La Fiction du politique* (Paris: Bourgois, 1987).

11. Martin Heidegger, *The Principle of Reason*, trans. Reginald Lilly (Bloomington and Indianapolis: Indiana University Press, 1991), p. 68: "Angelus Silesius, from whom we have already heard, can in his own way indicate Mozart's essence and heart through an ancient thought. Book 5, Fragment 366 from 'The Cherubic Wanderer' says: 'A heart that is calm in its ground, God-still, as he will/Would gladly be touched by him: it is his lute-play.'"

These lines, by which Heidegger solemnly renders homage to Mozart, are preceded by a long citation of a letter by Mozart in which he explains how composition took place in him. "Then it becomes ever larger and I spread it out ever more fully and lucidly, and the thing truly becomes almost finished in my head, even when it is long, so that afterwards I look over it with a glance in my mind as if it were a beautiful picture or a handsome man, and hear it in the imagination not at all serially, as it must subsequently come about, but as though all at once. That is a treat. Everything—the finding and making now proceed in me in a beautiful, vivid dream. But the listening to everything all at once is indeed the best" (p. 68). Heidegger's commentary makes one wonder if he doesn't summarize, in a particularly brutal way, the whole propos of philosophy on music: "Hearing is seeing." "Seeing" it all "in a single look" and "hearing thus all of it at once" are one and the same act. The unapparent unity of this seizing by sight and hearing determines the essence of thought, which was confided to us, other men, we thinking beings.

12. Martin Heidegger, *Nietzsche; Volume 1: The Will to Power as Art*, translated from the German by David Farrell Krell (San Francisco: Harper & Row, 1979), p. 80. (As with all the citations that I will take from this text, I am taking the liberty of modifying the translation to meet the needs of my demonstration.) [Krell's translation has been modified slightly here and below to match the French modifications.— Trans.]

(In many places, it is clear that the recapitulation that Heidegger undertakes of the history of the aesthetic, just like, further on, the interpretation he gives of "The Doctrine of Beauty in Kant," "responds" to the prehistory of the third *Critique* published several years before by the Rector Bäumler, one of the two most vehement official adversaries of Heidegger in the political years, the other being Krieck. See Bäumler, *Kants Kritik der Urteilskraft—Ihre Geschichte un ihre Systematik*, vol. 1 (the second volume has never been published) (Halle, 1923).

13. See in particular Martin Heidegger, *Introduction à la métaphysique*, trans. G. Kahn (Paris: Gallimard, 1967), pp. 153ff.

14. Martin Heidegger, *De l'origine de l'oeuvre d'art* (Première version 1935, texte allemand inédite), trans. E. Martineau (Authentica, 1987), p. 52; English translation from German by Werner Hamacher and David E. Wellbery.

15. Ibid. On originary *mimesis* and the apophantic character of *tekhnè*, I will take the liberty of referring the reader to my *L'Imitation des modernes* and "La Vérité sublime," in Jean-François Courtine et al., *Du sublime* (Paris: Belin, 1987); translated as *Of the Sublime: Presence in Question*, trans. Jeffrey S. Librett (Albany: State University of New York Press, 1993).

16. See Jacques Derrida, *De l'esprit—Heidegger et la question* (Paris: Galilée, 1987).

17. This is the title, from the Nietzschean lexicon, of a seminar co-organized by Heidegger in 1935 in Fribourg, which was without doubt the occasion of the first version of the conferences on the "Origin of the Work of Art" (1936).

18. See Heidegger, *Nietzsche 1*.

19. A bit further on, Heidegger undertakes the opposition of classicism and romanticism, apropos of the Nietzschean notion of the "grand style." But this opposition is of a typological nature, not doctrinal. Romantic theory of art apparently does not interest Heidegger.

20. Heidegger, *Nietzsche 1*, p. 104. I permit myself to refer to my essay "L'Antagonisme," in my *L'Imitation des modernes* (Paris: Galilée, 1986), pp. 113ff.

21. In general, Heidegger does not (re)translate *Sage* as *muthos*. It is only very late, in 1959, that Heidegger distinguishes the meaning of "legend" (*Sage*) (*On the Way to Language*, trans. Peter D. Hertz and Joan Stambaugh [New York: Harper & Row, 1971]); and even later, in 1962, he gives the equivalence *muthos-Sage* (*Aufenthalte*).

22. I will allow myself to refer the reader to my essay "Nietzsche apocryphe," in my *Le Sujet de la philosophie* (Paris: Aubier-Flammarion, 1979), pp. 75ff.

23. Nietzsche describes *Tristan*, in Chapter 8 of the fourth *Untimely Meditation*, "Richard Wagner at Bayreuth," as the "veritable *opus metaphysicum* of all art."

24. See Sylviane Agacinski, "Le tout premier écart," in *Les Fins de l'homme*, ed. Philippe Lacoue-Labarthe and Jean-Luc Nancy (Paris: Galilée, 1981), pp. 117ff.

25. Jacques Derrida, *Éperons, Les styles de Nietzsche* (Paris: Flammarion, 1978).

26. Here I am referring to the second of the lectures on "The Origin of the Work of Art," where this word, which would serve twenty years later to indicate the essence of modern technology, appears for the first time.

27. Heidegger, *Nietzsche 1*, p. 79. [The author's translation from Heidegger in the French text renders "Auseinandersetzung" as "explication"; Krell's English translation gives "confrontation." We have changed this translation to "differential explication," or just "explication." There is a semantic shadow of the agonal sense of "confrontation" in *Auseinandersetzung*, but in Heidegger it means "setting apart" and thereby opening a clarifying difference between two positions, such as those of two people conversing or a reader confronting a text.—Trans.]

28. E. Fink and M. Heidegger, *Héraclite*, French trans. J. Launay and P. Lévy (Paris: Gallimard, 1973), pp. 80–81.

29. See my "Typographie" and *La Fiction du politique*.

30. Heidegger, *Nietzsche 1*. For example, we know the famous defin-

ition of tragedy given in *The Origin of the Work of Art*: "In tragedy nothing is executed or represented [*auf- und vorgeführt*]; it is the combat [*Kampf*] between the new and the old gods that is delivered [*gekämpft*]."

31. Both "right" and "law" in this sentence are given as *droit* in the French text.—Trans.

32. Heidegger, *Nietzsche 1*, pp. 130–31. *Gesetz* is the word that Hölderlin uses to translate *nomos* in Sophocles or in Pindarus. It has the sense of a law of destiny for the gods as for men.

33. But all the same, *Kampf* is also used; we had one example. The euphemization of the Nazi lexicon or syntagma scarcely goes beyond ontological "diversion" or "revalorization." For example, in the discourse on the rectorship, "Blut und Erde" instead of "Blut und Boden." The difference as to meaning is perhaps huge. But what was one authorized—or encouraged—to understand in 1933 or 1936?

34. In my "La Vérité sublime," I tried to demonstrate the very profound inscription of the Heideggerian philosophy of art (and consequently of politics) in the "tradition of the sublime."

Chapter 4: Adorno

1. In *The Birth of Tragedy*, "culture of opera" or "civilization of opera" designate the "Socratic civilization" insofar as it is responsible for the (false) "renaissance" of tragedy in modern Europe from the sixteenth century at least until the neoclassicism of the end of the eighteenth century, itself impregnated with Rousseauism. What is incriminated here is the renaissance of a belated and inauthentic antiquity, a Hellenistic or—what is worse—Roman antiquity. Elsewhere I have attempted to show the immense political stakes of this dispute. See my *L'Imitation des modernes* (Paris: Galilée, 1986) and *La Fiction du politique* (Paris: Bourgois, 1987).

2. Cited in Theodor Adorno, *In Search of Wagner*, trans. Rodney Livingstone (London: NLB, 1981), p. 99. In the two passages cited here, Adorno quotes Richard Wagner, *Gesammelte Schriften*, 4: 127 and 130 [English translation, Richard Wagner, *Prose Works*, trans. W. H. Ellis (1892–99; reprint, New York: Broude Brothers, 1966), 2: 265 and 236. I have slightly modified the text of the published translation. The clause set off by dashes in the second quotation is missing both from Ellis's published translation of Wagner's works and from the English translation of *In Search of Wagner*.—Trans.]

3. Theodor Adorno, "Sakrales Fragment: Über Schönbergs *Moses und*

Aron," first published in his *Quasi una Fantasia* (Frankfurt a.M.: Suhrkamp, 1963). [The English translations provided here, sometimes in modified form, are from "Sacred Fragment: On Schoenberg's *Moses and Aaron,*" in *Quasi Una Fantasia: Essays on Modern Music,* trans. Rodney Livingstone (New York: Verso, 1992), pp. 225–48. Further references to this work will appear in parentheses in the text.—Trans.]

The intention to "save" (*retten*) the work is a critical motif that is already present in Benjamin's work, particularly in *The Origin of German Tragic Drama.* The *Rettung* ["saving"] consists in "mortifying" works in order to extract a second beauty from their ruins, a beauty that is an "object of knowledge." To save, in this sense, is to accede to the *Wahrheitsgehalt* of art works. Adorno applies this concept to "problematic" works, that is, to works that are the successful expressions of "false consciousness." See Walter Benjamin, *The Origin of German Tragic Drama,* trans. John Osborne (London: NLB, 1977), and Jean-Louis Leleu, "Présentation," in the French translation of Adorno, *Quasi una fantasia,* trans. J.-L. Leleu (Paris: Gallimard, 1982).

4. Martin Heidegger, *De l'origine de l'oeuvre d'art* (Première version 1935, texte allemand inédite), trans. E. Martineau (Authentica, 1987), p. 52; English translation from German by Werner Hamacher and David E. Wellbery.

5. Jean-Joseph Goux, *Les Iconoclastes* (Paris: Le Seuil, 1978). On many points I have allowed myself to be guided by the analyses contained in Goux's book.

6. This is not at all the case in Adorno's *Aesthetische Theorie,* ed. Gretel Adorno and Rolf Tiedemann (Frankfurt a.M.: Suhrkamp, 1970).

7. See Hegel's *Lectures on the Philosophy of Religion,* esp. section II-2.

8. Already in Longinus, the biblical pronouncement (as it happens, the *Fiat Lux* of Genesis) is a major example of a sublime utterance. On this subject, and on the subject of Kant, I will allow myself to refer the reader to my essay, "La Vérité sublime," in Jean-François Courtine et al., *Du sublime* (Paris: Belin, 1987); translated as *Of the Sublime: Presence in Question,* trans. Jeffrey S. Librett (Albany: State University of New York Press, 1993).

9. I will do this on the basis of what I tried to show in "La vérité sublime."

10. It is true that Adorno thinks that Kant's error is to have reserved the sublime for nature (see Adorno, *Aesthetische Theorie,* p. 496).

11. Immanuel Kant, *Critique of Judgment,* 52.

12. I have previously indicated that this formula is textually taken up by Heidegger in *The Origin of the Work of Art*.

13. See Adorno, "Sakrales Fragment": "Once someone asked Schönberg about an unperformed work, 'So you haven't heard it yet?' He responded: 'Sure I have, while I was writing it.' In such an act of imagination, the sensible becomes immediately spiritualized without losing any of its concrete nature. What is realized completely in the imagination thus objectively becomes a whole as a result, just as if the musical genius in Schönberg had completed the movement from the tribal gods to monotheism, whose story is condensed in that of *Moses and Aaron*. If the epoch refuses the sacred work of art, then, at its conclusion, it nonetheless releases the possibility under whose purview the bourgeois era began" (p. 475).

14. On this motif, which reappears often in Adorno's work (especially as regards Mahler), but which Adorno does not explain for himself, see O. Revault d'Allones, *Musical Variations on Jewish Thought*, trans. Judith L. Greenberg (New York: Braziller, 1984).

15. Hölderlin, *On the Translations of Sophocles*. In Benjamin's essay on Goethe, the caesura intervenes to justify the category of the "expressionless" [*das Ausdruckslose*], which Adorno continually refers to:

"The 'expressionless' is the critical power that, although it is not capable of distinguishing appearance from essence in art, nonetheless prevents them from commingling. It has this power in its capacity as moral word. In the expressionless, the sublime power of the true appears, just as it determines the language of the real world according to the laws of the mortal world. Namely, it destroys the last remnants of inherited chaos in all beautiful appearance: the false, mistaken totality—the absolute totality. It completes the work, which it smashes into shattered work, into a fragment of the true world, the debris of a symbol. A category of language and art, not of the work or of literary genres, the expressionless cannot be more stringently defined than Hölderlin defined it. . . . The 'Hesperian, Junonic sobriety' . . . is just another term for that caesura in which, along with harmony, every expression places itself in order to give space to an expressionless power within every artistic means." (Benjamin, "Goethe's *Wahlverwandtschaften*," in *Origin of German Tragic Drama*, pp. 181–82.) Benjamin situates the caesura of Goethe's *Elective Affinities*, understood in this sense, in one phrase, the one that "interrupts all the action": "Hope passed over their heads like a star that falls from the sky." In Goethe's novel, this phrase in fact seals the destiny of the heroes, Eduard and Ottilie, and all the more so because "they do not see it pass" (cited in Benjamin's essay, p. 200).

16. For more on this topic, see my *La Fiction du politique*, chap. 5.

17. See also Philippe Lacoue-Labarthe and Jean-Luc Nancy, "Le Peuple juif ne rêve pas," in *La Psychanalyse est-elle une histoire juive?*, ed. Adélie et Jean-Jacques Rassial (Paris: Le Seuil, 1981).

18. Adorno, "Fragment über Musik und Sprache," *Musikalische Schriften* (Frankfurt am Main: Suhrkamp, 1978), p. 252; English translation "Music and Language: A Fragment," in *Quasi Una Fantasia*, p. 2.

19. Walter Benjamin, "On Language as Such and on the Language of Man," in his *Reflections* (New York: Schocken Books, 1978), pp. 314–32.

20. Only at the moment of submitting this book to the editor did I become aware, through an associate, of the essay by Olivier Revault d'Allonnes, "Un Opéra profane de Schönberg: *Moïse et Aaron*" (*Revue d'Esthétique*, n.s., Privat, no. 8 [1985]), dedicated to Adorno. It seems to me from a first reading that, though arrived at by different paths, our conclusions are analogous.

MERIDIAN

Crossing Aesthetics

Philippe Lacoue-Labarthe, *Musica Ficta (Figures of Wagner)*

Jean-François Lyotard, *Lessons on the Analytic of the Sublime*

Peter Fenves, *"Chatter": Language and History in Kierkegaard*

Jean-Luc Nancy, *The Experience of Freedom*

Jean-Joseph Goux, *Oedipus, Philosopher*

Haun Saussy, *The Problem of a Chinese Aesthetic*

Jean-Luc Nancy, *The Birth to Presence*

Library of Congress
Cataloging-in-Publication Data
Lacoue-Labarthe, Philippe.
[Musica ficta. English]
Musica ficta: figures of Wagner / Philippe Lacoue-Labarthe;
translated by Felicia McCarren.
p.   cm. — (Meridian: crossing aesthetics)
ISBN 0-8047-2376-1 (alk. paper)
ISBN 0-8047-2385-0 (pbk.: alk. paper)
1. Wagner, Richard, 1813-1883—Influence.
2. Music—Philosophy and aesthetics.
I. Title. II. Series: Meridian (Stanford, Calif.)
ML410.W19L213   1994
782.1′092—dc20
94-15594
CIP   MN

∞ This book is printed on acid-free paper.
It was typeset in Adobe Garamond and Lithos
on a Macintosh IIci at Stanford University Press.